What's in your lunch?

BREAD
ON THE
WATER

Generosity without
condition or
expectation

DAVID W. POINDEXTER

WESTBOW
PRESS®
A DIVISION OF THOMAS NELSON
& ZONDERVAN

WestBow Press books may be ordered through booksellers or by contacting:

WestBow Press
A Division of Thomas Nelson & Zondervan
1663 Liberty Drive
Bloomington, IN 47403
www.westbowpress.com
844-714-3454

Scripture quotations are taken from the American Standard Version Bible.

Interior Image Credit: Helen O Williams

ISBN: 979-8-3850-2416-2 (sc)
ISBN: 979-8-3850-2418-6 (hc)
ISBN: 979-8-3850-2417-9 (e)

Library of Congress Control Number: 2024908550

Print information available on the last page.

WestBow Press rev. date: 09/19/2024

The American Standard Version 1901 is used as the scripture source in this series. It is one of the very few versions in the public domain. The common Bible translations are exceptional translations of the original Hebrew, Greek, and Aramaic into English. Each has its copyright.

(PapaDex version)
The (PapaDex version) is the authors' paraphrase of the 1901 ASV text. This is how he reads these scriptures to his grandchildren. Every scriptural quotation is paraphrased this way.

Each paraphrase reflects first century context, culture, and language for the reader while preserving the integrity of the original text. The author has a bachelor's degree in Bible, education and Theology. His master's in education, thirty-six years of marriage, and raising four daughters combine to lay an excellent foundation for communication with children and families.

To my dad
Thank you, Dad, for showing me what it looks like to live by faith and love the least of these, the invisible, those who live in the margins. In memory of B. J. Poindexter (August 19, 1939–December 10, 2019)

To my five best days
Thank you, Brenda, for a lifetime of grace. Since 1986, you've helped me become a better man one day at a time. I'm a better man because of you. The day we got married was my first best day.

The other four best days of my life are the daughters added to our tribe—Emily, Claire, Anne, and Ellie. Each one brings unique joy and pride to my heart as I watch you give away your lunch every day. You are my greatest teachers.

To our grandchildren, John David, Carson Bradley, Crocodile, baby g, and those yet to come
You are the reason I write. My prayer is that you continue discovering your faith in the One who created you. God gives you purpose in his story.

To my brother
You were my first and best friend. The core values in this series are ones we live as sons, husbands, fathers, and granddads. This writing effort is for your sons and their families as well.
In memory of Bradley Warren Poindexter
(January 15, 1968–June 2, 2023)

My prayer
I hope this story helps you know the heart of Jesus better. I hope you'll truly believe God has given you a lunch. He promises to make the most of everything you give Him, more than you could ever ask or even imagine on your own. Our heavenly Father is good, and He is generous. He is capable and He is willing.

Family on Purpose

A Series for Building Core Family Values

Each created story is inspired by true, first-hand accounts in Matthew, Mark, Luke, and John. Each miracle found in scripture stands on its own. This creative expression is similar to a songwriter inspired by scripture, creating lyrics that expand on the truth revealed in that scripture. This creative narrative is for instruction in righteousness and for encouraging fresh insight and deeper understanding. This is not an exhaustive list of values, but it's a good start.

> All Scripture is God's breath on a page and is inspired by Him. Scripture is profitable for doctrine, reproof, correction, and instruction in righteousness so that we will be thoroughly prepared for the good works which God has created for us. (2 Timothy 3:16–7)

How Does Family on Purpose Work?

Choose a core value that resonates

Commit to growth. Begin creating your family story and journal about it the next season. Just as an athlete develops muscle memory through repetition, you utilize the same principle with your core values. You strengthen what you use (good and bad) and that becomes your family's DNA. The more you use a core value, the more it becomes a natural part of your family's DNA. Adding additional core values each season deepens your family's story.

Read the story as a family

Read whatever way works for your family. Annotate, underline, comment, and reflect. Discuss the created elements and scripture.

Discover your place in God's story

Believe that your place in his story is beyond anything you can imagine or plan for yourself.

Cast your bread onto the water and trust him. Discover that he already has a place for you in his story. It's just waiting to be discovered.

Journal your journey

Each of the books in this series is only started. The second half of each book is designed for your family to journal your journey. *Bread on the Water* is not meant to be read and then put on the shelf. Each book in this series of field guides takes your family to a new place. It's a compass guiding your journey toward a greater purpose.

Repeat, pick another core value, and keep building

Continue journaling about your journey! In a decade, you'll have an amazing history of all that God has done. Family journals become like the growth charts in your pediatrician's office, charting your progress and milestones. When building families, the days drag on and the years fly by. Blink and children are grown. Don't just count the days. Make the days count.

Wheels up!   Let's roll!   Game on!   We got this!

Launch Lunch Finders and Family DNA Strategies

Every family has a unique DNA. It's a combination of individual gifts, passions, strengths and priorities. Every family is distinct because every family starts with unique raw materials. Unlike genetic DNA, you can choose and develop your family's DNA. You define and refine your family's core values and priorities, building on strengths and gifts, and refining excellence.

> By wisdom, a house is built.
> By understanding, a house is established.
> By knowledge, the rooms are filled
> with all precious and pleasant riches.
> Prepare for your work outside,
> Make your fields ready so you can get to work.
> Then, Build Your House
> Proverbs 24:3,4, & 27

CONTENTS

INTRODUCTION

Bread on the Water is a story about the generosity of one person to another. It just so happens that the one is a young boy and the other is Jesus. Though this story is a work of fiction, miracles of Jesus are true. His teaching, miracles, and parables are found in all four Gospels of the New Testament. These are the scriptures referenced in this story.

- **Feeding the five thousand**
  (Matthew 14:13–21, Mark 6:30–44, Luke 9:10–17, John 6:1–14)

- **Healing the woman who touched his robe**
  (Matthew 9:20, Mark 5:25, Luke 8:43)

- **Calling the two pairs of fishing brothers to follow Jesus**
  (Matthew 4:18–22, Luke 5:1–11)

- **Calling of Matthew and his dinner with Jesus and invited friends (other tax collectors and sinners)**
  (Matthew 9:9–13, Mark 2:13–17, Luke 5:27–28)

Jesus taught about one thousand days during His three years of ministry. Of those thousand days, the Bible records events that took place on only parts of fifty-nine of those days. The four Gospels only record thirty-seven of His miracles and thirty-nine parables during His ministry.

We don't know exactly how the ministry of Jesus unfolded over a thousand days, but I am confident that every element in *Bread on the Water* is consistent with His character and teaching.

> There are also many other things that Jesus did,
> If every one of them were written down,
> I suppose that the world itself could not contain
> All the books that would be written.

—John 21:25

> Cast your bread on the water, at just the
> right time, it will return to you.

—Ecclesiastes 11:1

BREAD ON THE WATER

Our Family Market

I sleep in my clothes every night, so I'm ready to go first thing in the morning. After the lamps are blown out, I get dressed in the moonlight and jump back in bed.

Sunrise sneaks over the mountains and across the rippling water so slowly. It's like the day will never start. As I catch that first whiff of Abba baking bread, I roll out of bed.

This morning, like every morning, I'm up the second the sun explodes across the water. Cool mornings next to the sea feel warmer with the aroma of bread baking in the marketplace.

Bread on the Water, our family's market, sits in the heart of our small village nestled by the Sea of Galilee. My abba's been baking bread since he was my size. He helped his abba bake bread for our village since, well, forever.

Just like my abba, I can't remember a time when I wasn't in the market, baking bread. Our community gave our bread ovens and storefront the official name, Bread on the Water. It's a constant reminder of God's faithfulness and generosity and how our family provides for our community.

Bread on the Water is packed every morning. All the bread is gone by noon. Jehovah Jireh provides our daily bread, but we bake it.

The market's new every day, yet it's the same all at once. I love it. Every morning, friends bring fresh fish, spices, vegetables, and treats to sell. Mom especially likes days when the fabric merchants arrive from afar. Their camels are loaded with colorful piles of beautiful cloth.

Some days are more fun than others. I love the days when the spice merchants come. That usually means something new and exceptionally yummy for dinner.

I have lots of small jobs around the market, but cleaning up after the camels is the worst. They make big messes from both ends if you know what that means.

Although I'm only eight years old, I know everyone. I know what all the vendors sell and what every neighbor likes to buy. Abba says that some people are easier to like than others, but we must do our best to love them all. He tells me, "Be nice to everyone regardless of how they treat you because they're the ones who butter our bread." I watch how my abba treats each person with respect and is nice to everyone, even to the mean ones. I do my best. I only grumble under my breath sometimes.

I love talking with friends and neighbors at Bread on the Water. There is always something to learn and a great story to share, even if it's one we've heard before. The more a story is told, the bigger the fish get.

A Place Where Friends Are Family

Abba says that Bread on the Water started with my grand abba baking bread for our family and a few friends. Eventually, our family began baking bread for most of the village. Over the years, there were some lean seasons when there was hardly any grain and only a little honey for baking bread. During those scarce times, our family had to choose between baking bread for just our family while friends went hungry, or sharing bread with neighbors so that everyone had a little. This was never an option we even thought about; being generous with others is who we are on the inside. We did not want to change that. Jehovah Jireh always came through. He always found a way, and we got to share in the joy.

> Cast your bread on the water,
> At just the right time, it will return to you.
> (Ecclesiastes 11:1)

One of the first things I remember Abba saying was this old proverb from the Torah. We chose to live by it every day: "Cast your bread on the water and in seven days it will return to you." Abba and Grand

Abba showed me this truth every day. I'm not sure why you throw good bread into the water when you're hungry, but I guess that's what they did. Everyone receives a little bread during the hard years, and we all eat like kings in the good years.

A little good bread shared with friends makes my stomach happy and my heart full.

In most seasons, the harvest and the honey are plentiful. Whether feast or famine, our neighbors make sure our family always has enough grain and honey for baking bread. Jehovah Jireh always provides. I learned to walk at Bread on the Water while carrying loaves of bread. Jehovah Jireh provided in every season before and every season since.

We use barley grain in our bread. The barley is grown in the fields near our village. We get a whole wagonload of barley grain for the same money as a few baskets of wheat grain. The wheat grain makes much tastier bread, but my family's special yeast and wildflower honey make the best bread, even using barley. At the end of each day, we grind grain for tomorrow's bread.

After grinding, mixing, kneading, baking, and selling our loaves in the market, we take all the leftover bread to families living by the shore. They are the outcasts. There are houses full of orphaned kids, lepers in their colony, and a couple of widows down the street. Somehow, there always seems to be just enough extra bread for Abba to share, almost like he planned it. Nothing goes to waste.

When we get home and open the door, the smell of tasty kabobs and hot bread fills the air. Dinner is ready. We start our meal by giving thanks to Jehovah Jireh, our provider. We still offer this simple prayer I learned as a tiny boy:

> Abba Father, thank You for today.
> Thank You for the food in my belly
> and the clothes on my back.
> Thank You for my family.
> Help me to grow up and be big and strong.
> Help me be full of wisdom and knowledge
> and common sense.
> Thank You for the promised Messiah.
> Our hope is in You. Amen!

Then we eat. We laugh and tell stories of our day in the market. It's perfect.

Abba then goes out to grind grain as I head to bed. I blow out the candle and get dressed for tomorrow. I kneel next to my bed, give thanks for the day, and jump under the blankets.

Now about the Fishing Brothers

Days in the market never really change, yet each one is never really the same. The fish selection depends on the luck of the four fishing brothers. These guys are really good. James and John are brothers. Their abba, Zebedee, taught them everything he knew about fishing. Simon and Andrew are also brothers, and they've been fishing with Zebedee for so long that he just treats them like sons. They know the lake better than anyone, and they know where to find the fish. If the brothers don't catch fish, then no one's catching fish. They always come back with the biggest and best selection.

These brothers have been a band since they were way smaller than me. Over the years, they got into plenty of trouble because of their mischievous adventures. They have the scares to tell their stories. James and John were given the nickname "sons of thunder" by their neighbors. These four love each other and make each other better men. Smoking fish over a beachside fire is their favorite time together. I need my own band of brothers.

My First Friend

Andrew is my first and oldest friend. Even though I'm only eight, he treats me like a man. We talk about fishing and everything else. Every time we're together, we laugh till we cry. My first memory of him was when I was five years old, walking in the market. I knew from that first day we would be fast friends for life. I also know that he's loved me from the beginning.

When Peter, Andrew, James, and John haul their morning catch into the market, Abba opens the bakery and people begin to swarm. I wonder what's in their nets today.

The Grumpy Tax Collector

"Boy! Hey you, boy!"

I don't have to see his face to know who is calling for me. It's Matthew, the tax collector. He knows my name is David but refuses to use it. I wonder if all his money makes him grumpy or if he was just born grumpy.

"Get me the two best from the brothers' catch!"

I swallow hard and remember Abba's words: "Every customer is the butter for our bread." I go to get his fish.

I race across the market, jumping over baskets of figs and olives and dodging camels and goats. When I round the corner, I see the four brothers' tent is empty. There are no fish to buy. It will be interesting to tell Matthew that his money can't buy everything! He gets the funniest faces when he doesn't get what he wants before he gets mad.

I find Abba and ask if the brothers had a bad night. Abba chuckles and explains, "The boys all quit this morning to follow the Jewish carpenter turned teacher. They just dropped their nets and left. So ole Zebedee is back in the boat this very minute, mending nets."

I've got to see this for myself. I race to the shore and discover their boat on the water's edge, nets left behind, waiting to be mended. The four brothers are gone.

I asked a man from another boat about what he saw. He replied, "The teacher walks up to them and says, 'Follow me and I will make you…'" His voice trails off as I turn and run back to the village.

Mamaw
April 12, 1943 – August 20,2022

꒳ DAVID W. POINDEXTER ꒳

My Dear Friend Anna

Abba hands me a bag and says, "This food is for Anna. Please take it to her and ask if she needs anything else. This can't wait until this evening." The bag contains bread and small fish.

It's been hard not seeing Anna in the market anymore. She used to find me and gently touch my shoulder. She was so quiet coming up behind me; she would nearly scare me out of my robe. She always teased my abba about how much he was paying me and always gave my hand a squeeze when she left for home. Lately, she never leaves home. Her body has grown weak, and her gentle touch is just a memory.

Abba faithfully checks on her at home to make sure she has enough food and helps out where needed. She has an ornery goat that's good company but is constantly making messes. I miss her voice and gentle touch. I only see her when we drop off bread. She has an amazing joy in her heart that I just can't understand.

Her body has been sick for such a long time, but that has made her kindness even brighter. She's like the morning sunshine. Her smile says joy. As I watch her struggle and her body weaken, she regularly reminds me that the joy of the Lord is her strength! I looked that up later in the Torah. The rest of that writing gives the reason: "And now He has become my salvation." She reminds me every visit about our hope in the coming Messiah.

Anna creates small gifts with messages of hope using cloth remnants and ink. She gives these priceless gifts to friends on their special days of celebration. Each one is a treasure. I have a few of her treasures in a small box beside my bed. She makes everyone feel known.

Matthew's Party

"David, David! Can you do me a big favor?" I turn my head and look because the voice is familiar, but the kindness is strange. It's Matthew. He says, "I need a big favor and I know that you're the only one willing to help me. I'm throwing a party tonight for my friends and I need some help getting food together."

My shocked face gives me away. Matthew laughs. "Yes, I have friends. They're the other tax collectors and the rest of the people your parents warn you not the hang out with." I am speechless, almost. Without even thinking, I ask "Why?" Matthew turns, takes a slow breath, and says, "The teacher from Nazareth came into my office today and invited me to follow Him."

After a long silence, Matthew looks me in the eyes and says softly, "He's giving me a second chance. I can start over … Like new. What I've done doesn't bother Him. So please spare no expense on the food, my friend, and thank you."

Smiling, I walk away, thinking about the four fishing brothers and Matthew all in the same boat. This must be some teacher. I've gotta see for myself.

The Meantime

Days in the village are sure different without the four brothers and Matthew. Zebedee's getting back in the swing of fishing. The grandkids are learning, and Grand Abba is enjoying teaching. They spend the days mending nets and, in the wee hours of the morning, fishing. They've gotten pretty good in a very short time.

Life seems to have found a new normal. I keep on helping merchants unload their baskets of treasure and cleaning up after their camels.

I'm always listening for news of the four brothers and Matthew. This teacher is doing unbelievable miracles and telling amazing stories. I reach to move a basket of olives and the memory of a gentle touch on my shoulder feels almost real. I turn, and to my surprise, I see Anna. She is back in the market, and she is completely well!

"How?" I whisper.

Anna quietly replies, "I heard that many have been healed by just His word or His touch. A huge crowd gathered in front of my home as the teacher from Nazareth was passing by. The crowd was so large, I could not see Him. I knew I'd never make it to the shore to hear Him, and I was not allowed in the temple. I waited for Him to pass right by me. As He passed by, I reached for the hem of His robe. Immediately, I was healed, my strength was back, and my body was like new."

Anna continues, "He stopped and turned. I was so scared at first. It's the gentleness of His smile peeking from behind that curly beard that settled my racing heart.

"Jesus said softly to me, 'Your faith has made you well, Anna.' Can you believe it, David? The teacher, Jesus from Nazareth, knows my name. He is the Messiah."

My mind races with one single thought, *I have to see Jesus for myself.*

Andrew Comes for a Visit with Friends

The days drag on forever as they turn into weeks. Finally, one morning, Zebedee tells me that the boys will be coming by today and that Jesus is with them. I ask Abba if I could go, and he says, "Yes, but only after my work is done." I work harder than ever until all that's left is cleaning up after those nasty camels.

The crowd is gathering on the grassy hillside just outside the village, and Jesus is already teaching by the time Abba finds me. He tells me the camels can wait, but hearing the teacher will not. He tosses me a bag with some bread and fish inside. I remind him, "Anna doesn't need this anymore because the teacher—"

Abba interrupts, "I know Jesus healed her. It's your lunch, pal. Enjoy the day. Tomorrow will be a long, hard day of traveling to fill our empty grain baskets in the morning and then baking."

I run as fast as I can and find a place near the teacher, thanks to my old friend Andrew. Words can hardly describe Jesus. His voice is almost like Abba's. Anna is right about His smile. He teaches like no one I have ever heard. Even as a kid, I understand Him.

Every single person listens to every word because He speaks to us as friends, telling stories about the kingdom of God. It isn't until I see the mountain shadows chasing the sun across the lake that I realize my stomach is rumbling. I've listened to Jesus teach all day without even thinking about eating. Apparently, so has everyone else. But now, stomachs are rumbling all over the place.

Jesus keeps talking with new friends while the four brothers are busy trying to figure out a way to feed five thousand men and their families. I look at the lunch Abba has given me. I hear my stomach rumble, then I listen to my heart.

I grab Andrew and whisper that I want to give my lunch to Jesus so at least He can eat. He's been teaching and healing all day long and has to be hungry and tired. Andrew just smiles. He rubs my head, grabs my hand, and takes me to see Jesus.

He keeps whispering to himself over and over, "This is perfect. Thank you!"

As I get close, Peter stops me and says to the others, "This boy's abba runs a local market. We can get food there."

This Is Plenty

As Peter and the others try to figure out the cost, Jesus walks over to see me and Andrew. He just smiles. I tell Him, "There is no bread to buy this late in the day. The market is empty. Here, You can have my lunch."

Jesus puts His hand on my head, gathers me in His arms, and says "Thanks, David. This is just right and this will be plenty."

The voice in my heart says, "He knows my name just like He knows Anna's."

He turns and asks the crowd to sit in groups and then he invites us to bow our heads. The hill is silent except for the blowing grass. He lifts the barley loaves into the air, breaks them, and gives thanks to Jehovah Jireh, our provider. As we open our eyes, we discover the miraculous.

The stones at our feet have become bread. The baskets near the shore are now filled with fish ready to eat. Jesus keeps breaking the barley loaves and filling baskets for the disciples to distribute among the people. Everyone shares in the bounty.

As the crowd learns of a young boy's generosity, they too begin to share with their neighbors the small portions of food they've brought. Olives, figs, and grapes begin to appear as moms make sure everyone has some. Soon, a simple banquet breaks out all over the hillside. Andrew leans over and says with a mouthful of fish and bread, "That's what we call fishing."

This miracle started with a small humble gift. Jesus blessed it, broke it, and then multiplied it. Five loaves cast on the water fed five thousand families. This is bread on the water!

Twelve Baskets Full

I'm too excited to eat. I just want to be close to Jesus. And then, at that very moment, our eyes connect across the crowd, and He motions for me to come over. He says, "I need some empty baskets and wonder if you know where I can find some."

I tell him that my abba has some at his market. He asks, "Would you mind going to get them?"

I grab a couple of friends, and we turn to race for home. "As many as you can," are His last words. We are gone and back in no time.

When everyone has eaten their fill, Jesus directs that each of his disciples pick up a basket and collect the extra bread and fish. Even after feeding thousands, each disciple brings back a basket full of food. Jesus looks at me and asks, "Any ideas on what we can do with all this extra food?"

I know in an instant that with Abba covering my chores today. There is no time to bake extra bread for the widows and families by the shore. I ask if we can take the baskets of food to them. Jesus just smiles and says, "Good thinking, my friend." Off we go to find my abba at Bread on the Water with twelve baskets of food.

We find him in the market just as he's finishing up with those nasty camels. I introduce Abba to Jesus.

"Hello, Joseph. My name is Jesus. You have a remarkable son."

I tell the incredible story about giving my lunch to Jesus and the miracle of Him multiplying the bread and the fish, collecting twelve baskets of leftovers, and talking with Jesus on our short journey here all in a single breath.

Abba kneels down on one knee, looks me square in the eye, and says, "Son, you cast your bread on the water, and in just the right time, it has returned to you." Abba tells Jesus about our hungry neighbors, and we leave right away to pass out the food. There is more than plenty! Nothing is wasted in His kingdom.

Nothing Is Wasted in His Kingdom

Jesus and the disciples turn and start heading back to the shore. As I'm watching, Jesus turns around and starts walking backward. He locks eyes with me, smiles through that curly beard, and then winks. As He turns back around and catches up with the disciples, all I can hear is Jesus whistling and the disciples laughing.

Abba and I turn toward home.

What an amazing day!

All Dressed and Ready for Bed

The moon is bright as I look across the water. I wash my face, hands, and feet. I get dressed for tomorrow and get into bed. I don't want to close my eyes because I don't want this day to end. As I said, no day in the market is the same, but this one was truly amazing.

I met Jehovah Jireh, our provider.

I met the Messiah who called four fishermen from our village to follow him. They gave up their life's work to find their greatest purpose.

I saw the smile and felt the touch of the one who gave Anna her life back.

I see why Matthew threw a party for his friends and why he invited Jesus, and I know why Jesus went.

I introduced my abba to the Messiah.

I discovered Jesus could do a lot more with two small fish and five loaves of bread than I could.

I look back on this amazing day, and all I can think about is that He knew me long before I ever met Him.

I understand now that Bread on the Water is more than our family business; it's the miracle Jesus let me see with my own eyes.

As I close my eyes, I can still feel the teacher's touch on my head. My heart swells when I remember how grateful He was when I gave Him my lunch.

I know tomorrow starts way too soon, but my heart will not go to sleep. I blow out the candle anyway.

Before Sunrise

The sun's glow is barely sneaking over the mountains, stretching across the lake. Today, as always, I'm dressed and ready to go, but it's much earlier than usual. There is no amazing smell of Abba baking bread because, first, we need to buy grain at Abram's farm. Last night, after dropping off the extra food, we loaded our empty baskets onto the wagon. This morning, our first task is already done before we even start the day. Abba always thinks ahead.

I try to turn the wagon and hitch our stubborn donkey, but neither will budge. Why won't the wagon move? I try again with all my strength before giving up and going to get Abba. When we come back, our donkey is waiting patiently, eating some grass. He just wants breakfast before work.

Abba tries to move the wagon, and it barely budges. He looks in the back at the baskets, then looks at me, and then looks back in the wagon at the baskets. "Did you happen to look in the baskets this morning, David?"

As I pull myself up to peek over the side of the wagon, the sunrise explodes over the lake to show me twelve baskets full of golden wheat grain pressed down, shaken together, and running over.

He did it again!

Jehovah Jireh is our provider, and He is my friend.

The end of this story is the beginning of your story

Message in the Miracle

This young boy trusted Jesus at the invitation of a friend, Andrew. The boy was generous, giving without condition or expectation. He didn't give his lunch to Jesus so it could miraculously feed five thousand men and their families. He gave his lunch for Jesus to eat. He had no idea that Jesus would do anything more with his humble gift than eat it.

The young boy cast his bread onto the water. His humble generosity is so powerful that feeding the five thousand is the only miracle found in all four Gospels of the New Testament.

We live in a time where our focus is on the epic, going viral, and being shared and liked by hundreds or thousands. We want to ensure the maximum impact of our efforts and our gifts. We have a genuine desire to be generous, but we also want to ensure our gift multiplies. The more we try and leverage our impact, the less we leverage His.

This miracle is about one person who trusts Jesus with all that he had on this one day. A boy's only concern is placing his gift in the hands of

Jesus. Barley loaves are bread for the poor. Jesus shows us what humble generosity looks like when He blesses and multiplies our gifts.

The wholehearted generosity of a child is so profound and critical in the kingdom of heaven's faith that Jesus says, "Unless we have the faith of a child, we cannot enter the Kingdom of Heaven" (Matthew 18:3).

Generosity without condition or expectation is love in its purest form. That's why Jesus came, to give His life for yours. He gave with no condition or expectation. He invites you to believe and be saved in this life and for eternity. He also invites you to remember His generosity with a meal, which includes bread. We call it communion.

Questions For Good Conversation

1. What is the difference between child-like faith and childish faith?
2. How are gratitude and generosity connected?
3. Where have you seen God multiply a little into miraculous?
4. Jesus said, "I am the bread of life, anyone who eats will live." What does this miracle about giving bread to everyone say about the Kingdom of God?
5. Who will do more with your lunch, you or Jesus?
6. What is holding you back from trusting him with your lunch?

Feeding the Five Thousand
A Harmonization

The Four Gospel Accounts

It is important we remember that this miracle is recorded in scripture and is the only miracle found in all the four Gospels. Four unique perspectives of the same miracle are written to four unique audiences. This harmonization takes all four perspectives and creates a single, comprehensive story.

- Matthew 14:13–21
- Mark 6:30–44
- Luke 9:10–17
- John 6:1–14

Jesus needed to get away from the crowds. After learning from the disciples that John the Baptist was killed, he needed to mourn the loss of his good friend and cousin. He directed the disciples to find a boat and withdraw to the town of Bethsaida by sailing to the other side of the Sea of Galilee. They all needed time at this desolate place for rest and food.

Many people saw them sailing, and soon, a large crowd gathered along the shore to follow them. They followed Jesus because of all the healing and miracles He was doing for the people. From the boat, Jesus could see the great crowd gathering. Passover was at hand. When He landed on the shore, He welcomed them and spoke of the kingdom of God. He had compassion for them because they were like sheep without a shepherd. He began to teach them many things. He healed the sick. He restored the broken. He welcomed the misfits.

When evening was approaching, Jesus said to Philip, "Where are we to buy bread so that these people may eat?" He said this to test him, for He knew what he was about to do.

The disciples came to Him and said, "This is a desolate place, and it is late in the day. Send the crowds away into the surrounding countryside and villages and buy food for themselves."

Jesus said, "You don't need to send them away. You give them something to eat."

Looking up and seeing that a massive crowd was coming toward Him, Philip answered Jesus, "Two hundred denarii worth of bread would not be enough to buy food for each of them to get a little."

Then Jesus said, "What do you have?"

One of his disciples, Andrew, Simon Peter's brother, said to him, "There is a boy here who has five barley loaves and two fish, but what are they for so many?" There were about five thousand men and their families on the hillside.

There was a lot of grass in that place. Jesus invited the crowd to sit down in groups of about fifty. Jesus accepted the gift of the young boy's lunch, all five loaves and two fish. He looked up to heaven, gave thanks, and said a blessing over the food. He divided the fish and loaves among the disciples. Somehow, this small gift multiplied, and every single person ate until each one was satisfied.

As they finished eating, Jesus instructed each disciple to grab a basket and collect the leftovers so that nothing would be lost. Twelve baskets of leftover fish and barley loaves were collected in all after feeding five thousand men and their families. When the people saw the miracle, they said, "This is indeed the prophet who has come to save the world."

Special Thanks

Thanks to my alma mater, Cincinnati Christian University (formerly Cincinnati Bible College), class of '85. Our gospels professor, Richard Foster taught us this study technique, and it's been an incredible study tool over my life. We learned to take multiple perspectives from the Gospels and combine them into a single narrative giving us a more complete picture. When we tell our own stories, we include details that are pertinent to our unique audience. This is what the writers of the Gospels did. Harmonization gives us all the perspectives and details combined.

GOOD THINKING!

Questions for Inquisitive Minds and Good Conversations

Good Thinking!

Questions for Inquisitive Minds and Good Conversations

1. Scripture, clinical research, and common sense all conclude that a leading cause of joy and happiness is humility and gratitude. Generosity is the fruit of this heart position. How can you develop a heart of humble gratitude every day?
2. The author has embedded many of his family's core values into the story. Can you look back and identify some of them?
3. What are the core values in your family?
4. Does generosity mean I have to give all my food away?

   [] Yes
   [] No
   [] All of the above. Explain how both are true.

5. What is the cause (s) of "unkindness?"
6. What is the antidote of "unkindness?"
7. Will you launch this 30-day adventure into Gratitude?

Project: Thirty Days of Gratitude. Each family member identifies one specific thing that you're grateful for every day for the next thirty days. Make a composite family list on Post-it notes. The more specific, the better. Try to identify something new every day.

Dad Joke: How does an ant move a bag of rice?

One grain at a time!

8. How does this awful dad joke relate to small acts of kindness leading to change in your community?

Good Thinking!

Questions for Inquisitive Minds and Good Conversations

1. What does kindness look like?

Here are a few examples of generosity through small acts of kindness:
Look people in the eye
Smile
Wave
Address people by their first name (on their name badge)
Say "Good morning,"
"Have a good day,"
"Goodbye," and
"Thank you."
(Learn these phrases in a new language every week)
Tip well.

2. What are your ideas for expressing generosity through small acts of kindness?

-
-
-
-
-
-
-

Good Thinking!

Questions for Inquisitive Minds and Good Conversations

1. What are your habits of kindness?

2. How would your day be different if you saw it as God's generosity toward you?

3. Another word for generosity is sharing. What are thr blessings you currently have that you could share?

4. Another word for generosity is hospitality (the same root word in hospital). How can you care for people?

5. How does the response of Jesus to the boy's generosity impact what's in your hands?

6. How does Andrew's interaction with the young boy give clarity to the role of parents, guardians, teachers, or coaches?

7. God promises you that He will deliver above and beyond (pressed down, shaken together, running over the top) when you give with a whole heart. Where have you seen this?

8. Jesus could do no miracles in His hometown because of their disbelief. What is the relationship between belief and God moving?

Good Thinking!

Questions for Inquisitive Minds and Good Conversations

1. How is every single person a coach?

2. Coaching is more than just athletics. If you are in a position to influence, you are a coach. If you lead, mentor, teach, encourage, inspire, or have any contact with people, you are a coach. A horse-drawn coach moves people from place to place. This is exactly what a human coach does, you move people from place to place. With a plus, minus, or zero, evaluate how you move people from place to place.

3. How are people better after having connected with you?

4. How do you become more intentional in leading as a positive coach?

5. How is God's blessing and favor connected to our belief and obedience?

6. Generosity is your response to grace not the price for grace. Jesus calls you to action in response to grace, not the condition for receiving grace. How do you love others from a place of being fully loved?

7. How do you prepare for generous opportunities?

    "Luck in the intersection of preparation and opportunity" – John Wooden

Good Thinking!

Questions for Inquisitive Minds and Good Conversations

1. You are saved when you believe and call on His name. Is there a moment in time when you have received His forgiveness for your past, grace your future and the promise of God's presence in your life today? Tell someone about it.

2. What does "the grace you extend reflects the grace you've received" mean?

3. The boy gave his lunch to Jesus because he thought Jesus would be hungry. Why do you think this gift was so powerful and profound to Jesus and the gospel writers?

4. The boy did not give from his excess or his leftovers. He gave everything he had at the exact moment it was needed. How do you recognize these opportunities? What can you give away?

5. How is generosity more than giving money and a lunch?

6. What are the small acts of kindness you can start today?

7. What did Jesus mean when He said, "If you've done it for the least of these, you've done it for me"?

8. What did Jesus mean when He said, "If you've given as much as a cup of cold water in my name, you've given it to me"?

Good Thinking!

Inquisitive minds have their own questions, what are yours?

_____

_____

_____

_____

_____

_____

_____

_____

_____

_____

_____

_____

_____

_____

_____

_____

Questions for Grandparents

1. Who were the people in your family who have a legacy of generosity? Gratefulness? Intentionality?

2. What are their stories?

3. How can you demonstrate generosity (beyond gift-giving) to your children and grandchildren?

4. What does child-like faith look like in your twilight years?

5. Your children and grandchildren learn the most when the things you say and the things you do are consistent. What did you get right?

6. We need to make this course correction immediately...

7. What do you want your children and grandchildren to say about you when you're gone? (This is your hope and prayer)

8. What will they say about you when you're gone? (This is your legacy)

9. What can you start doing today that turns hopes and prayers into reality?

JOURNAL

Generosity
Without Condition or Expectation

Our Family Story
Casting our Bread on the Water

Our Family

_____

Our Family Was Established on

_____

Journal Starting Date

_____

Our Family Story of Generosity

Casting bread upon the water is an expression that means to give generously without expectation or condition. God's story begins like this, "For God so loved the world he GAVE." (John 3:16).

The greatest story ever told is about *giving*. His grace is free to all who believe. He offers joy in the journey, peace in the storm, purpose in the plan, and strength in the struggle. He invites you to cast all your fear, anxiety, and worry on Him. When you humble yourself and accept His gift, He shoulders the load for you and promises to go with you always.

More than that, God promises that our gifts in His hands will be blessed and multiplied beyond what we could ever ask or imagine or generate on our own. No gift in God's hands is too small.

In response to His grace ...

- We live with humble gratitude, remembering every gift is from God.
- We start today living purposefully as a generous family.
- We trust God as we discover our place in His story.
- We journal our journey. Nothing replaces old-school writing.

Caution!
This journal of generosity is not a scorecard or highlight reel. By remembering well in a journal, you're able to come back later and reflect on what God has done with your humble gifts. When you release generosity into God's hands, with no acclaim, the focus is on generosity and not the giver. You entrust others to see goodness and glorify your Father in heaven.

"Do this in remembrance of Me"—Jesus

Jesus instructs us to remember His greatest gift by breaking bread with each other in the sacrament of communion. He's not requiring our gratitude. He's inviting us to remember and treasure His sacrifice, the moment He traded His life for yours. When you're generous, you're reflecting an understanding of this priceless gift of life you've been given. We love others as He has loved us. You don't give from guilt or obligation or for acclaim; you give because He gave first. Generosity is your response to His grace. I've witnessed it. You will be a witness.

There is genuine joy in giving

Start being generous and journaling about the humble gifts you've placed in God's hands. You may never know how God uses your gifts until you get to heaven. That's okay. That's why Jesus invites us to store up treasure in heaven. Sometimes, God winks and gives us a peek at how He uses and multiplies our generosity. There is unspeakable joy found in giving generously, unconditionally, and without recognition. Try it!

Our brains are amazing

As you begin to focus on a *certain thing*, that certain thing starts showing up way more often than it used to. This is a cognitive bias or a frequency illusion. It's not that a certain thing starts appearing more often; it's that your brain is paying more attention to it. When you start to be generous and journal about generosity, you begin to discover more opportunities to be generous. You create ways to be generous. This certain thing, aka generosity, starts with a single first step. It becomes a habit and then develops into second nature. Generosity purposely becomes part of your family DNA.

Jesus teaches, "The kingdom of God is like … A man plants mustard seed, the smallest of the garden seeds. He watches it grow over the decades to provide shade and rest for all the birds of the air. A woman takes a little yeast and puts it in big baskets of grain meal. Over time, the entire grain mixture is proofed and ready to make hundreds of loaves of bread" (Luke 13:18–21).

Your family is invited to plant seeds of love, joy, peace, patience, kindness, goodness, and faithfulness. You're called to cultivate, nurture, and protect these fruits in your family.

Your family is invited to become the "yeast" in your community.

In this season, our family is baking sourdough bread. Feeding the starter, discard, proofing, bannetons, have become the everyday lingo of our homes.

All it takes to make amazing bread is some "starter" and a willing heart. Adding starter to pancakes, waffles, pizza dough, and … you get the picture. It only takes a little starter to make something truly amazing. All it takes to change a neighborhood, a classroom, a school, or a community is a little "generosity starter." That's God's promise and His plan!

You are his plan.

You are his starter.

First Journal Entry

Our Promise

Today's date: _____

We will cast our bread on the water and live generously by

- expressing gratitude; remembering that every gift is from God;
- walking humbly and trusting God as we discover our place in His story;
- living purposefully as a generous family;
- tracking in our journal the good things that God has done through our family; and
- releasing the blessing as we place no conditions or expectations on our gifts.

We will "seek justice, love mercy, walk humbly with our God" (Micah 6:8).

Wholeheartedly,

(everyone signs their name)

BREAD ON THE WATER   39

Reflecting
The times we got it right

Look back across the years and generations in your family. Every family has times and traditions of generosity. Sometimes it's obvious, sometimes it's more challenging. This part of the journey is important as you remember well and remember together. You'll discover things that you missed or have been totally oblivious to that parents and grandparents, aunts and uncles did. They didn't make a big deal of it, but their generosity was intentional. Remember well. Remember together.

You may discover times of generosity, giving without condition or expectation. You may discover times of giving, but it came with conditions and expectations.

The focus of reflecting is on the action, not the motivation. Make observations, withhold judgment, extend grace, and celebrate the wins. Remember the times you got the giving part right. If you can also identify the times when giving came without condition or expectation, even better, celebrate their generosity.

It is very difficult and subjective to look back and assign motivations. So let's not get lost in that rabbit hole. Reflect on your history of goodness and kindness. Write your story.

Our Family of Origin

Family pics

Reflect

We got it right!
Honor the generosity of previous generations by sharing their stories.

_____

_____

_____

_____

_____

_____

_____

_____

_____

_____

_____

_____

_____

Reflect

"Whatever you do in word or action, do it in a way that points to God."

_____

_____

_____

_____

_____

_____

_____

_____

_____

_____

_____

_____

_____

Reflect

We got it right!
Honor the generosity of previous generations by sharing their stories.

_____

_____

_____

_____

_____

_____

_____

_____

_____

_____

_____

_____

_____

_____

_____

Reflect

"Whatever you do in word or action, do it in a way that points to God."

_____

_____

_____

_____

_____

_____

_____

_____

_____

_____

_____

_____

Reflect

We got it right!
Honor the generosity of previous generations by sharing their stories.

_____

_____

_____

_____

_____

_____

_____

_____

_____

_____

_____

_____

_____

Reflect

"Whatever you do in word or action, do it in a way that points to God."

_____

_____

_____

_____

_____

_____

_____

_____

_____

_____

_____

_____

Reflect

We got it right!
Honor the generosity of previous generations by sharing their stories.

_____

_____

_____

_____

_____

_____

_____

_____

_____

_____

_____

_____

_____

Reflect

"Whatever you do in word or action, do it in a way that points to God."

_____

_____

_____

_____

_____

_____

_____

_____

_____

_____

_____

Our Family of Choice
Family pics

Breaking New Ground
We got it right today!

Starting today, this is our new story of generosity, giving without condition or expectation.

Write your story of goodness and kindness. These are your treasures in heaven. These moments become the jewels in your crowns, crowns that you cast at the feet of Jesus who is on the throne reigning for eternity.

Our only motivation:

Be a Mirror
Whatever you do in word or action, do it in a way that when people see your actions, they glorify the Father in heaven. When the boy gave his lunch, people did not focus on the boy's gift. Five thousand families remembered the generosity and provision of Jesus.

Be Salt and Light

- Be the touch that adds extraordinary flavor to every conversation and action.
- Preserve the goodness of the moment and the goodness of God in every person.
- Illuminate God's grace and the path to finding hope, joy, peace, freedom, life, and Jesus!

Be the "Starter" in your home and community

Breaking New Ground

We got it right, Today!
Our stories of Generosity, loving others like we've been loved.

_____

_____

_____

_____

_____

_____

_____

_____

_____

_____

_____

_____

_____

Breaking New Ground

We are the salt of the earth! We are the light of the world!

_____

_____

_____

_____

_____

_____

_____

_____

_____

_____

_____

_____

_____

_____

Breaking New Ground

We got it right, Today!
Our stories of Generosity, loving others like we've been loved.

_____

_____

_____

_____

_____

_____

_____

_____

_____

_____

_____

_____

_____

Breaking New Ground

We are the salt of the earth! We are the light of the world!

_____

_____

_____

_____

_____

_____

_____

_____

_____

_____

_____

_____

_____

_____

Breaking New Ground

We got it right, Today!
Our stories of Generosity, loving others like we've been loved.

_____

_____

_____

_____

_____

_____

_____

_____

_____

_____

_____

_____

_____

Breaking New Ground

We are the salt of the earth! We are the light of the world!

_____

_____

_____

_____

_____

_____

_____

_____

_____

_____

_____

_____

_____

Breaking New Ground

We got it right, Today!
Our stories of Generosity, loving others like we've been loved.

_____

_____

_____

_____

_____

_____

_____

_____

_____

_____

_____

_____

_____

Breaking New Ground

We are the salt of the earth! We are the light of the world!

_____

_____

_____

_____

_____

_____

_____

_____

_____

_____

_____

_____

_____

Breaking New Ground

We got it right, Today!
Our stories of Generosity, loving others like we've been loved.

_____

_____

_____

_____

_____

_____

_____

_____

_____

_____

_____

_____

Breaking New Ground

We are the salt of the earth! We are the light of the world!

_____

_____

_____

_____

_____

_____

_____

_____

_____

_____

_____

_____

_____

_____

_____

Breaking New Ground

We got it right, Today!
Our stories of Generosity, loving others like we've been loved.

_____

_____

_____

_____

_____

_____

_____

_____

_____

_____

_____

_____

_____

_____

Breaking New Ground

We are the salt of the earth! We are the light of the world!

_____

_____

_____

_____

_____

_____

_____

_____

_____

_____

_____

_____

_____

_____

Breaking New Ground

We got it right, Today!
Our stories of Generosity, loving others like we've been loved.

_____

_____

_____

_____

_____

_____

_____

_____

_____

_____

_____

_____

_____

_____

Breaking New Ground

We are the salt of the earth! We are the light of the world!

_____

_____

_____

_____

_____

_____

_____

_____

_____

_____

_____

_____

_____

_____

Breaking New Ground

We got it right, Today!
Our stories of Generosity, loving others like we've been loved.

_____

_____

_____

_____

_____

_____

_____

_____

_____

_____

_____

_____

_____

Breaking New Ground

We are the salt of the earth! We are the light of the world!

_____

_____

_____

_____

_____

_____

_____

_____

_____

_____

_____

_____

_____

Whatever you do in word or action,
do it in a way that gives glory to God

We are salt that gives good flavor and preserves.
We are light that points people to Jesus

EPILOG

Hindsight and Insight

IOW: How Do We Become Wise?

Hindsight is 20/20

This old expression comes from your optometrist. It means that your eyes see at twenty feet what healthy eyes see at twenty feet The expression refers to looking back across your personal history and discovering that some of it makes sense in the present. We discover the why in the what. This can be true for both brokenness and blessings. Usually, hindsight is associated with an unfortunate outcome that might have had a different result if we had known then what we know now. You can become paralyzed by "should have," or you can learn and be better next time. That is hindsight.

When hindsight is discovered, we say things like, "Ah, now I see that this was given for a specific purpose of blessing others." Or we say, "That was the most difficult thing I've ever experienced. I don't want to ever go through it again, but I learned ..." In this process, we discover wisdom and understanding. You build on what you did right and change what you got wrong. Wisdom is taking hindsight and improving the "next time."

Other times, things from the past still don't make sense in the present. We hope that it will make sense someday or trust that it will all eventually make sense in eternity. Wisdom and understanding can be found at these crossroads.

Looking back, you need to exercise caution because you only see history from your perspective, which is different from another's perspective. That seems obvious, but it's not always instinctive. Humble hindsight can lead to others gaining similar insight.

The *Oxford Dictionary* defines *hindsight* as a noun
>   hind·sight
>   /ˈhīn(d)ˌsīt/
>   *noun*
>   understanding of a situation or event only after it has happened or developed.
>   "**In hindsight**, I should never have gone."

***Hindsight* is also a verb and an adverb**
>   *verb*
>   1.   hindsight is the process of understanding a situation or event after it has happened with the intention of becoming wiser and growing stronger through it.

>   *Adverb*
>   Responding to your family history is qualified in one of three ways:

>   1.   **Should've and could've** is the static way of looking back with regret and getting stuck in past mistakes or brokenness.

>   Failure is your story.
>   Grace is your release.

2. **Nostalgia** is a healthy reflection on the best of your past. It becomes unhealthy when you stay there or try to replicate it. There's an unspoken fear that the future will never be as good as the past.

   Fear is your story.
   Believing that in His story the best is yet to come is the key to your freedom.

3. **Next time** is the process of becoming wiser by looking back, celebrating the wins, and learning from the failures. Regardless of the outcome, you press on toward greater things.

   Growth is your story.
   You live your best possible life in God's story.

Purposeful hindsight is the key to wisdom and understanding
When you choose a growth mindset, you take an honest look at the past. You wholeheartedly celebrate the wins. You take an honest look at your mistakes, and you learn from them. You make amends, seeking forgiveness and restoration where possible. You make course corrections in behavior and processes. You humbly move forward with greater humility, wisdom, and understanding. Jesus says, "As far as it is possible, be at peace with all men." However, sometimes that is just not possible, and you need to move forward regardless. He also said, "Shake the dust from your feet." Wisdom is found in recognizing the tipping point.

Learn from your mistakes
An old friend, Joe Ehrmann says,

> "It's not the mistakes in life that matter.
> It's what you do with what you learn from those mistakes."

When you don't change your behavior as a result of failure, there is no learning. It's just failure. The end. Full stop!

This does not have to be the end, ever. You can learn from a mistake you made last week or a mistake you made twenty years ago. It is never too late to learn from your mistakes and change your behavior. Maybe you've learned from the mistake, and you're still holding onto the shame. Make it right as best as you can. Seeking forgiveness and extending grace are powerful forces in gaining wisdom and peace. Then move forward.

Better yet, learn from the mistakes of others
Wisdom is learning from the mistakes of others because this learning comes with no consequences or punishment. Hmmm ...

Best ever, learn from the success of others
Wisdom is learning from the success of others and using that as a catalyst for your own adventures. There's a direct connection between risk and reward. The young boy who gave his lunch away heard amazing stories of others who had powerful interactions with Jesus. Their lives were changed forever. He needed to see for himself. The young boy didn't know what Jesus would do with his lunch. He just wanted to share it. His risk was being turned away and eating his own lunch or being successful and going hungry until dinner. To a hungry boy, lunch is priceless. The cost was real, and the risk was worth it.

Insight

The characters in Bread on the Water are based on people from my childhood in LeRoy, Illinois. I grew up in this small farming community in the middle of the state. My dad, Joseph "BJ" Poindexter, was a partner with his uncle Prier in the town grocery store. Poindexter's IGA was *the* marketplace. Everyone—young, old, rich, and poor—needed to eat, and they found their groceries at our IGA Foodliner. My dad made sure everyone had food. This book is in honor and memory of him. He lived for eighty years.

As I read through the manuscript for the thousandth time, I realize I use the term "my dad" a lot. I changed "Dad" to "Abba" because this is the most tender expression of the father/child relationship in Jewish culture. My heart breaks for those who can't look back on their childhood and be proud of their dad or, in some cases, even know their dad. Your past brokenness does not determine your future. Your current brokenness does not determine your future. It shapes it.

If you're a son of an abusive, broken, or absent father, know that his behavior was not your fault. Become the father you desired to have. Be an amazing father to your children. Stop the cycle. Renew the generation.

If you're a daughter of an abusive, broken, or absent father, know that you are created to be cherished and loved. Anything short of that is not your fault.

These may be the wisest words I've heard about our fathers:

> "Our earthly father is a reflection of our heavenly Father.
> Our heavenly Father is the perfection of our earthly father."
> Louie Giglio, Passion City Church, Atlanta

I wish it were true that every dad tries to get it right. Mine did most of the time. For the times he didn't, I extend the same grace he gave me. Dad loved me first. I loved him back. Sounds familiar?

The picture above shows the IGA store employees of 1965 when I was two years old. BJ is second from the left. Uncle Prior is on the far right. Every Thanksgiving and Christmas morning, BJ would open the store for at least one family missing an important part of their meal. This was back in the day when all business was closed for holidays. When neighbors offered to pay, Dad wished them "Merry Christmas!" These priceless gifts of butter or milk made their celebrations complete. That was his joy. BJ offered jobs, credit, and grace. He affirmed dignity and walked with integrity.

Our family went with less so we could share with others. We ate barley bread while he gave others wheat bread. Still, we ate like kings.

When a can of food got dropped and dented, it couldn't be sold. He kept these cans in a ready place for families with immediate needs. Nothing was ever wasted. Boxes of canned goods were routinely given away.

Every person mattered to BJ. Every customer who bought groceries provided the "butter for our bread." He would repeat that phrase during the hardest moments. The money from kind people and grumpy people all paid our bills. We treated everyone with kindness regardless of how they treated us. We saw our dad do that every day of his life.

Dad showed us how to build bridges, not burn them. As far as it is possible, don't leave a relationship in ruins. You never realize in the kingdom of God where God will choose to use an old bridge to make a new connection. You can't cross a bridge you've burned.

Anna reminds me of a beautiful 4'8" eighty-year-old grandma and friend of our family, Mrs. Killian. Mrs. Killian lived in LeRoy, Illinois, and made it her mission to get me paid more than twenty-five cents an hour working at the IGA when I was eight years old. My new bride and I would visit with her over the last decade of her life when we went back to LeRoy. She was a kind soul who walked with Jesus and treasured His friendship to the end of her days.

Matthew, pre-Jesus, reminds me of my uncle Prier. He was not a bad person. It just seemed that most of the time, he valued money over relationships and things over people. My dad made sure everyone ate. Uncle Prier made sure everyone paid. But that wasn't his entire story. My uncle and aunt never had children of their own. Instead, they adopted his nephew and raised him as their own. Uncle Prier always made his prized new Cadillac available for our prom dates. My brother and I were so appreciative of his generosity. I don't know if my uncle ever got to know Jesus personally. I only know that he saw Jesus every day in my dad and that Uncle Prier was loved to the end.

My dad was not perfect, but he loved the people Jesus saw—the people everyone else misses, the people hard to love. He died in

December of 2020 in the middle of a global pandemic. I've been working on this story for the better part of two decades. I needed to cast my own bread on the water and submit *Bread on the Water* for publication. I submitted the manuscript to the publisher on the third anniversary of his passing.

Dad had been in the hospital for a few weeks with congestive heart failure and was released to go home and be the grand marshal of the LeRoy Christmas parade. On the ride home, he enjoyed a chocolate milkshake while Rodney Atkins sang "I've Been Watching You."

He walked into the home he helped build fifty years ago and sat down to rest in the garage where he lost consciousness. We carried him to his bed where he quietly passed a few hours later while holding my mom's hand as she lay beside him. The last song he heard on earth was "The Goodness of God" by Bethel Music. It was a fitting tune to be whistling as he met Jesus face-to-face.

He never liked being the center of attention, so watching the parade from heaven suited him just fine. The community was wonderful, honoring him with black drapes in the empty grand marshal's convertible. It was fitting and beautiful. LeRoy is a small town at its finest.

Writing *Bread on the Water* is my humble attempt to honor my dad's "casting bread on the water" faith. My dad always gave thanks for Jesus and the salvation we have through Him. He is right: miracles happen *as we give thanks*.

The child's prayer over the meal is from my brother Brad. He prayed this prayer every meal with his three sons. My nephew, Brad's middle son Zach Poindexter, helped me get it right. Brad's men still pray this prayer over meals with their own children. Brad lost a brief and brutal battle with cancer in June 2023. He was my first and best friend for fifty-five years. We were the iron that sharpened the other. We laughed until we cried every time we talked. It was always the best medicine. He is missed. I honor him and the strong faith he has passed on to the next generations.

With this story, I hope that our children and grandchildren see that we are all created in the image of our generous Father in heaven. I hope the same for your children and grandchildren. We are invited to be part of His amazing story. Jesus loves each of us in spite of our failures. He will receive and bless the smallest humble gift.

I am nothing without His grace. Apart from Him, I cannot bear good fruit. I can do all things through Christ who gives me strength.

Here was my lunch. I'm casting my bread on the water.

What is a nudge?

The nudge to act
Sometimes you get a feeling in your heart to do something kind, to be extra generous, or respond to a need. That could be God's spirit inviting you into His story of loving others. The young boy of this story acted on a nudge by offering his lunch to Jesus. Andrew was the lunch finder because he was looking up and saw the boy.

When was a time you got a nudge and then moved on it?

The nudge to reach out to someone
There are moments, out of the blue, when someone's face comes to mind. It could be concern or gratitude. This is likely a nudge, or a kick in the pants, to reach out. Don't ignore it. When you walk with God, He brings people to mind for a reason.

When was a time you got a nudge to reach out to someone and then reached out?

I missed a nudge, and it is my greatest regret
My single greatest regret in working with students over the past thirty years happened on a Sunday morning when going into worship service. Getting four daughters ready and on time was a constant challenge. We were running just behind time, and I needed to get seated with my family. I noticed one of our high school students sitting alone outside of the sanctuary. The nudge was to stop and check in with him, but the pull was to be on time. I said hello and headed into worship. When we came out, he was gone.

Later that night, we got a call that he had taken his life. He had come to church to say goodbye. I missed the nudge. It is the single greatest weight that Jesus carries for me. Every day since, with grace, I listen and act on nudges.

OUR FAMILY DNA

A journey of discovering who we are
and who we can become

Generosity
Gratitude
Grit

Adventure
Creativity
Purpose
Mindful
Obedience

Best
Clarity

We are His workmanship, created in
Christ Jesus to do good things.
That's His only plan from the beginning.
Life is a gift, go live it!
(Ephesians 2:10)

Family DNA

/ˌdēˌenˈā/
noun

1. Genetic DNA is a self-replicating material that is present in living organisms as the carrier of genetic information. It contains the fundamental and distinctive characteristics or qualities of someone or something.
2. Family DNA is a self-replicating, self-creating, self-refining adaptive culture in families of choice. It contains the fundamental and distinctive characteristics or qualities of the family which include strengths, gifts, passions, talents, vision, mission, and heart of each one. Each one is both a carrier and creator of family DNA.

Every family is unique

Every chromosome in your body contains DNA carrying your distinctive characteristics and qualities. The same concept is true for the unique characteristics and qualities in your family of origin. Your unique family DNA is passed along from generation to generation. The family you came from is your family of origin. You can't change what you were born into or the culture you were raised in. Just like in mapping our genetic DNA, if you can discover what went wrong, you can take the steps to avoid replicating brokenness in future generations.

You have the amazing opportunity to determine what broken things you'll leave behind and what good things you'll keep. This is called your family of choice.

You create your family DNA. You define your purpose, values, practices, and priorities. You define the strengths, standards, values, qualities, and characteristics of your family DNA. You will adopt and adapt DNA from your family of origin as you also generate new and unique family DNA in your family of choice.

Defining the distinct characteristics, values, and qualities in your family of origin is an important starting point in refining your family DNA moving onward. When you choose to combine your family of origin DNA with another person's, a totally fresh and unique family DNA is generated in your family of choice.

Characteristics, values, and qualities from each one's family DNA are self-replicating in your new family, both good and bad. Families have the amazing opportunity to start fresh. New characteristics and qualities are also created. What would it look like if you purposed to define and refine your family DNA from the start?

Begin with an intentional focus on three choices:

1. Choose to replicate the goodness you've known.
2. Choose to replace the brokenness you've experienced.
3. Choose to discover and create the uniqueness that will define your family DNA.

Replicate

the goodness you've known

What are the qualities and values from your families of origin that you want to replicate in your family of choice? You determine the values and goodness that get carried into your family, as well as what gets left behind. Adopt the goodness you've known into your family. You have the flexibility to adapt and customize what you bring, creating a hybrid.

Example:

Sunday Suppers–If getting the family together for a big Sunday meal was special in your family of origin, and you agree that you want that tradition to be in your future, then choose to make it a priority in your family of choice.

Examples of family traditions:

- Holidays,
- Vacations,
- Meals,
- Birthdays,
- Faith Practices

Now you think of some:

-
-
-

Replace

the brokenness you've experienced

Every family of origin has "things you didn't get right." As a result, we've all experienced some degree of brokenness. Sometimes, these negative patterns of behavior in your family of origin result in significant brokenness and a fear that even if you promise you'll never repeat the damaging behavior, you inevitably will.

The great news is brokenness is not destined to be repeated. You can leave it behind, walking forward with your family of choice by replacing brokenness with goodness. A word of caution, your past only stays behind when you replace it with new positive patterns.

> Bless the Lord with your whole heart.
> Let everything within me, bless His name
> Bless the Lord with your whole heart.
> Remember God's faithfulness.
> He pardons your rebellion and failures.
> He heals your disease.
> He redeems your life from hopelessness.
> He crowns you with lovingkindness and compassion.
> He satisfies your years with good things.
> He renews your youth like an eagle.
> The Lord is compassionate and gracious,
> Slow to anger and abounding in lovingkindness.
> (Psalm 103)

You must recognize and replace the brokenness, or it will be repeated. Restoring the brokenness to wholeness is not automatic; it must be intentional and will be challenging. You can't restore yourself. The Lord is compassionate and gracious.

There are some brutal and damaging events in so many of our stories. The consequences of broken trust and abuse follow us and continue to steal our innocence. Faith, family of choice, and wise counsel are critical in the healing and restoration process. There are also some amazing counselors and therapists who are highly skilled and compassionate in all areas of family therapy. Be courageous and reach out. Sometimes casting our bread on the water means reaching for the rescue lifebuoy.

A Transitional Character

"A person, who, in a single generation,
changes the entire course of a lineage.
Who somehow find a way to metabolize the poison and
refuse to pass it on to their children.
They break the mold.
Their contribution to humanity is
to filter the destructiveness out of their lineage
so that the generations downstream will have
a supportive foundation upon which to build productive lives."

Dr. Carlfred Broderick, PH. D

With God's strength, you can be the one!

Originate

fresh family DNA

The miracle of marriage is profoundly more than a ceremony and a license. There is something immeasurably stronger created when two individuals start their lifelong process of becoming one in a wedding ceremony before God and witnesses. The covenant of marriage is when two individuals become one. In their family of choice, they discover and create their own unique family DNA. This single event begins the lifelong process of two becoming one, defining and refining your family DNA.

Refine

what you discover

Excellence is a persistent heart position of getting better, stronger, and wiser. Mistakes, setbacks, failure, and loss are part of every journey, but they are not the end of the story. A growth mindset continues a trajectory of excellence. Celebrate achievement and accomplishment. Drive an anchor and hold the gains as you press forward. Learning is a lifelong pursuit. Precious metals become more valuable as they are refined. The same is true of character, skills, and strengths.

Hope Is Grounded in Truth

Hope is recognizing that a positive outcome is possible. Defining hope for your family is the genesis of a healthy and growing family DNA. Start with this small first step. Put your hope into words. Miracles are dreams made manifest. Hope realized starts with writing out what is possible.

Our hope is ...

At the end of today,

At the end of this week,

One year from today,

One decade from today,

When I am gone, this will be my legacy,

A Great Start

Reverse engineer your legacy

You'll leave a legacy, good, bad, or indifferent. What are you going to leave behind when you're gone? Start by defining the end you desire, then work your way backward to the present. What if every small decision, action, and choice takes you in the direction of your end game?

If that sounds impossible, that's because it is. Life is hard and unpredictable. You can't anticipate the challenges, roadblocks, losses, or wins. Be encouraged. You can equip your family with the character needed to realize your inherent excellence. You can develop resilience and find the wisdom to negotiate any challenge, fully realizing the potential you're created with.

Great families don't just happen by accident; they develop on purpose with intention, action, sacrifice, wisdom, and resilience. Defining your legacy is not a question to answer on the corner of the page or even a whiteboard flowchart on the garage wall. If the thought of creating a legacy of hope and excellence for your family feels overwhelming, that's because it is! When you look at the lifetime responsibility of leading your family well, you will get discouraged and lose heart if you try and do it alone.

Encouraging News

You don't have to do it on your own

You are not created to do it on your own. That's an impossible pressure. Doing it alone exceeds the manufacturer's design specifications for a family. We are created to grow stronger in community and with the blessing and favor of God.

Truth Never Changes

Scripture is our foundation in the storm

> We make plans, but the Lord directs our steps. (Proverbs 6:9)

> Where there is no vision and plan, there is chaos. (Proverbs 29:18)

> Seek first the kingdom of God and the most important things in life will be added to you. (Matthew 6:33)

> Trust in the Lord with all your heart. Don't lean on your own understanding. In every decision and action acknowledge him, and He will direct your path. (Proverbs 3:5–6)

> Seek justice, love mercy, and walk humbly with God. (Micah 6:8)

> Delight yourself in the character and presence of God and He will give you the desires of your heart. Commit your way to the Lord and trust in Him because He will deliver. He has been faithful. He will always be faithful. He's the same God, then and now. (Psalm 37:4–5)

The *Best* News

You don't have to write your own story, you're already in His

The pressure is off. You are created to be part of His story. Your family already has a place of promise in the greatest story ever. This doesn't mean that you join the team and do nothing. Our creator invites you into meaningful relationships and authentic purpose. He invites you into discovery, adventure, and trust. It is only within His story that you'll discover all that you're created to be.

From the beginning, God created mankind in His own image, breathing His own breath into man. God's image and His breath separate man from every other created thing. He invites your family into His story.

> Follow Me and I will make you… (Matthew 4:19)

Lunch Finders

Family DNA

Hundreds of people followed Jesus as He began teaching, including the twelve who were eventually called to be His disciples. From all those who followed, the twelve were invited to discover their greatest purpose. This same invitation is open for you and your family today. Discover your place in His story. He already has more for you than you could ever dream of or imagine on your own. In His story, you'll find life, meaning, peace, and hope.

It starts with you answering a very simple question, "What's in your lunch?"

The Most Important Question for Your Family

What's in your lunch?

The boy in the miracle of feeding five thousand gave Jesus his lunch with only five loaves and two fish. It was all he had for the day. He gave without condition or expectation. It was all Jesus wanted.

Every person has a lunch. We're not talking about bread and fish, but a combination of gifts, strengths, passions, skills, core values, and abilities. Each member of your family and circle of family influencers has a lunch. Take a close look at what's in each person's lunch. Look for their gifts, strengths, passions, skills, and abilities. What are the values they hold dear that can help shape your family into what you hope for?

What would it look like if we offered our lunches wholeheartedly without expectation or condition?

Then encourage our circle of family influencers to do the same. We build each other up.

This young boy's gift was not spectacular because it fed five thousand men and their families. It was spectacular because it was all he had and offered at the exact moment he felt the nudge in his heart to give without condition or expectation. He gave his lunch to feed one person, Jesus. That's the childlike faith Jesus asks of us.

On these next few pages, identify the stakeholders in your family. A stakeholder is any person who has a place or influence within your family, starting with parents and children. Can you even imagine how much stronger your family would be if you tapped the strengths of every person in your circle?

Every single person on the planet is a *lunch finder*! We can all discover and build greatness in others. Jesus found greatness in the generosity of a boy giving his lunch away. Know what's in your own lunch and then help others discover what's in their lunch.

Family DNA

Essential Wisdom for Parents

Be Humble

"There is no pride in authorship. I don't care who gets the credit for our school corporation graduating exceptionally strong students and extraordinary people. Excellence is our goal. We will be strong in every way. It takes community" (#strongineveryway Dr. Scott Robison, former superintendent of Zionsville Community School Corporation).

It Takes Community (verb)

"A community" has a longitude and latitude on the GPS and a population sign as you enter and a "thanks for visiting" sign when you leave. It can also be a smaller part of a large city. Building strong families requires significantly more than the just the village that surrounds them.

Community is not geography. It is not a location or a collection of people. It is not a person, place or thing. It can't be found on WAZE.

Community is a culture of belonging. Community is where inspiration and challenge meet grace and encouragement. Respect is earned and extended. Excellence is honored and expected. Creativity and failure are fresh starts. Community connects faith, strengths, purpose and talents across generations, building compounding human interest. Humility and gratitude give rise to forgiveness and redemption. Community is where you discover you're part of an eternal story bigger than yourself. When Jesus prayed in John 17:21 that, They would all be one," this is as close as I can imagine to what he means.

It takes community to build quality families. As parents and guardians of our children, it is our responsibility to raise quality citizens and people. That doesn't mean we have to do it alone. Truth be told, we can't do it alone.

When we humbly come to this reality, we begin to invite others of kindred spirit to come alongside. They join this great calling of leading our children to maturity. My wife and I were very intentional about bringing other adults into our children's lives—those who are kindred spirit in faith, working hard, pursuing excellence, having a greater purpose, loving God, and loving others.

Who are your people of kindred spirit?

Who influences your family?

Who is building life into your family?

Grandparents?

Aunts, uncles, and cousins?

School teachers?

Youth and small group leaders?

Coaches?

Parents of friends?

Pastors?

Mentors?

Others?

There is a common belief that you become like your five closest friends. That is only part of the story. Your community of influence is far broader than just these five individuals. Every single person from the previous list has influence. You will be influenced by those you hang out with so choose wisely. The simple truth is confirmed in Proverbs.

> "Walk with the wise, grow wise ... a companion of fools suffers harm" (Proverbs 13:20).

Become Lunch Finders

Concentric Circles of Influence

Start here.

Your innermost circle is your immediate family. What's in everyone's lunch?
Consider using personality inventories from work or school, character strengths assessments, enneagrams, coaching evaluations, and teacher evaluations. Maybe you could even ask one another at the dinner table?

When taking inventories and surveys there is a tendency to answer them as the person we aspire to be and not who we genuinely are. With a humble heart, answer as you are. You will discover who God made you to be. Every person is unique. Take the time to learn from inventories. More importantly, discover the treasures around your own dinner table.

In your journal, each person gets their own lunchbox. Be as detailed as possible.

Next
Who are the three to five *consistent daily* influential people in each of your lives?
What's in their lunch? (because that's what they're building into you)

Then
Who are the five to ten *weekly* influential people in each of your lives? Maybe choose two.
What's in their lunch? Fill in their box with as much detail as possible.
(at this point, you may be out of boxes – add more sheets!)

Then
Who are the *seasonal* influential people in each of your lives?
What's in their lunch?

Who are the *single/annual event* influential people in each of your lives?
What's in their lunch?

Any person who has influence in building life into your family should have their own lunchbox.

Caution, there may be some negative influencers who you need to distance and protect your family from. Be wise and courageous. Who do you need to remove?

What's in your lunch?

Name:
strengths, skills, passion,
values, gifts, known for...

Name:
strengths, skills, passion,
values, gifts, known for...

We are His workmanship, created in Christ Jesus to do good things. Ephesians 2:10

What's in your lunch?

Name:
strengths, skills, passion,
values, gifts, known for...

Name:
strengths, skills, passion,
values, gifts, known for...

We are His workmanship, created in Christ Jesus to do good things. **Ephesians 2:10**

What's in your lunch?

Name:
strengths, skills, passion,
values, gifts, known for...

Name:
strengths, skills, passion,
values, gifts, known for...

We are His workmanship, created in Christ Jesus to do good things. Ephesians 2:10

What's in your lunch?

Name:
strengths, skills, passion,
values, gifts, known for...

Name:
strengths, skills, passion,
values, gifts, known for...

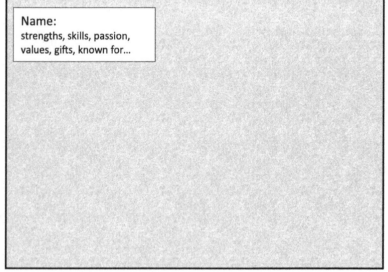

We are His workmanship, created in Christ Jesus to do good things. Ephesians 2:10

What's in your lunch?

Name:
strengths, skills, passion,
values, gifts, known for...

Name:
strengths, skills, passion,
values, gifts, known for...

We are His workmanship, created in Christ Jesus to do good things. Ephesians 2:10

What's in your lunch?

Name:
strengths, skills, passion,
values, gifts, known for...

Name:
strengths, skills, passion,
values, gifts, known for...

We are His workmanship, created in Christ Jesus to do good things. **Ephesians 2:10**

⊰ DAVID W. POINDEXTER ⊱

What's in your lunch?

Name:
strengths, skills, passion,
values, gifts, known for...

Name:
strengths, skills, passion,
values, gifts, known for...

We are His workmanship, created in Christ Jesus to do good things. Ephesians 2:10

What's in your lunch?

Name:
strengths, skills, passion,
values, gifts, known for...

Name:
strengths, skills, passion,
values, gifts, known for...

We are His workmanship, created in Christ Jesus to do good things. Ephesians 2:10

⋅≼ DAVID W. POINDEXTER ≽⋅

What's in your lunch?

Name:
strengths, skills, passion,
values, gifts, known for...

Name:
strengths, skills, passion,
values, gifts, known for...

We are His workmanship, created in Christ Jesus to do good things. Ephesians 2:10

What's in your lunch?

Name:
strengths, skills, passion,
values, gifts, known for...

Name:
strengths, skills, passion,
values, gifts, known for...

We are His workmanship, created in Christ Jesus to do good things. Ephesians 2:10

What's in your lunch?

Name:
strengths, skills, passion,
values, gifts, known for...

Name:
strengths, skills, passion,
values, gifts, known for...

We are His workmanship, created in Christ Jesus to do good things. Ephesians 2:10

What's in your lunch?

Name:
strengths, skills, passion,
values, gifts, known for...

Name:
strengths, skills, passion,
values, gifts, known for...

We are His workmanship, created in Christ Jesus to do good things. Ephesians 2:10

What About an Empty Lunch Box?

Maybe this is your confession, I feel that I don't have anything worth sharing? Maybe you've been hit with a devastating event leaving you crumbled and lost with a crushed heart? Maybe, you've been running on empty for a long time?

If this is your reality, I have great news.

Jesus came with grace and truth. He promises to be with you always and he still brings grace and truth. He loves you where you are. He loves you too much to leave you there. We need to remember the rock-solid foundation of truth.

> **Truth is stronger than feelings.**
> **Truth never changes regardless of feelings.**
> **Truth is the same yesterday, today, and forever.**
> **If truth changes, it never was.**

This Is Truth

Beauty from Ashes Is God's Promise

> Jesus fulfills the prophecy of Isaiah 61:1–3 by saying, "The Lord has anointed me to bring good news to the hurting. He has sent me to bind up the brokenhearted, to proclaim freedom to the captives and freedom to prisoners, to proclaim favorable the year of the Lord, to comfort those who grieve" (Luke 4:18–19).

Where Do I Turn in My Brokenness?

> I lift up my eyes to the hills, where does my help come from? My help comes from the LORD, the

Maker of heaven and earth. He watches over us constantly. He will neither slumber nor sleep. (Psalm 121:1)

When I turn my head to the left or the right, I may not see you, but I hear your voice from behind me saying, keep moving forward, this is the way, I'm walking with you. (Isaiah 30:21)

He sees our every need and will take care of us. He gives us rest beside quiet water. He restores our hearts. He walks with us through the valley of death and grief. (Psalm 23:1–4)

The Lord is a shield protecting us. He lifts our heads showing us hope. (Psalm 3:3)

Humble yourself before the mighty and gentle hand of God. He will lift you up at the proper time. Give all your fear, anxiety, and brokenness to Him and He will carry it because He cares for you without condition. (Peter 5:6–7)

When You're in the Eye of the Storm

He is with us in the storm, He is our unshakable foundation.

Sometimes He stills the storm in us.
(Matthew 7:24–27)

Sometimes, He stills the sea.
(Luke 8:24)

Sometimes, He just rides out the storm with us. (Matthew 8:23–24)

Sometimes, He calls us to walk on the water. (Matthew 14:23–31)

Redundancy in Scripture Means Pay Attention!

"Behold"
Look up, look around, look and see.
Found 1,500 times in the Bible.

IOW: look up from your screens!

You'll never see the movement of God around you when looking down at your screen.

You'll never receive or give encouragement to the person next to you if your eyes are down.

What if you traded one day's screen time (the average is 5 hours) each week for "beholding" God, the people next to you, family, your spouse, your children, roommate, nature?

What if you kept your phone in your pocket when walking to and from anywhere?

What if everyone in the car went "hands free" and not just the driver?

Behold! Discover what you've been missing!

"Fear not, Don't worry, take heart, be courageous."
Found 365 times in the Bible.

IOW: Where do we place our trust?

Who is worthy to trust with your story?

Better yet, what will it look like when you trust that your story is already embedded in God's story?

He sees you. He knows you. He has a purpose and a plan for you.

He calls you his own, so you don't have to go it alone?

You don't have to carry the weight of the world on your shoulders. Jesus already did.

What if We're Broken?

I am broken. I am struggling and my hope is fading. You are in the right place. The most broken people in the ministry of Jesus are found broken hearted at his feet. What is His response?

> Jesus was walking by the Sea of Galilee and saw two brothers, Simon Peter and Andrew fishing. Then, Jesus said, "Follow Me, and I will make you fishers of men." They caught so many fish the boats began to sink. Simon Peter fell at His feet and confessed that he was a broken and unworthy man. (Luke 5:1–10)

> Great multitudes came to Him. They were lame, blind, deaf, maimed, and afflicted. Friends laid down their brokenness at the feet of Jesus and he healed them. They all marveled. (Matthew 15:30)

> Jesus met everyday people giving them hope, saying, "Rejoice!" They held his feet and worshiped Him. (Matthew 28:9)

> Jairus, a ruler of the synagogue came to Jesus and fell at His feet because his daughter was sick to the point of death ... do not be afraid any longer, only believe. (Mark 5:22)

> A woman whose young daughter was possessed by an evil spirit came and fell at His feet ... Jesus spoke ... when she returned home, her daughter was free. (Mark 7:25)

> A prostitute came into the house of a prominent Pharisee and sat at the feet of Jesus while he was

reclining at the dinner table. She brought an alabaster flask of expensive fragrant oil and began to wash His feet with her tears and wiped them dry with her hair. She kissed His feet and anointed them with the oil. (Luke 7:37–50)

Mary sat at the feet of Jesus listening to Him teach, even as her sister, Martha, got mad for neglecting her meal—hosting chores. Jesus speaks of Mary having chosen the good part. (Luke 10:39)

Mary came to Jesus and fell down at His feet, crying to Him, "Lord, if You had been here, my brother would not have died." Jesus cried as his heart broke. (John 11:1–35)

One of the ten healed lepers returned and fell at the feet of Jesus and glorified God. (Luke 17:11–19)

The man who was demon possessed, shackled, cutting himself, naked, living in the tombs was now free, healed, clothed, in his right mind, sitting at the feet of Jesus. (Luke 8:26-40)

A woman found Jesus and touched the hem his robe. She was healed. Her last hope is Jesus. She is welcomed with compassion and healing. (Luke 8:47)

The woman caught in adultery was thrown at the feet of Jesus. Broken, guilty, and condemned. She is helpless without hope. Jesus meets her at the worst and last moment of her life. But Jesus does not leave her there. He places himself between her and the mob bent on killing her. Jesus loves her enough to meet her at the worst moment of her life and loves her so much that he gives her the option to start over again, she is free to start a new life. (John 8:1–11)

On the night before the final week of his life, Mary, the sister of Martha and Lazarus, knelt at the feet of Jesus. That evening, she anointed his feet with a fragrant oil that filled the whole house. She washed his feet with her hair. Jesus says, "Truly I say to you, wherever the gospel is preached in the whole world, what this woman has done will be spoken of in memory of her." (Matthew 26:6–13, Mark 14:3–9, John 12:1–8)

After the crucifixion and burial, the disciples' hearts were broken, and hope was lost. They hid together and waited. Suddenly, Jesus just showed up and asked, "Why are you troubled? Why do you have so much doubt in your heart? Look up, see my hands and my feet, take a close look at my scars. It's me in the flesh." (John 11:2)

Brokenness meets grace at the feet of Jesus.

Hope is found here.

Family DNA: Action 1
Clarifying Our Vision

What is your family vision today?

What is your family all about in a single sentence?

What is your family vision that fits on a coffee mug?

What is your family vision that can be spoken as the car door opens in the morning carpool line?

Family DNA: Action 1 (DIY lab)

Creating Our Family Vision

How to Create Your Family Vision
As a family

1. List all the things your family wants to be.
   - one idea per notecard or Post-it note
   - as many as you can think of
   - nothing out of reach
   - you can add ideas as you go
2. Spread all on the ideas table or wall.
3. Read every single one of the ideas.
   - no judgment
   - no lectures
   - no shade
   - smile
   - learn
   - every idea is important to one member of the family
4. Group the ideas, one by one, into common-ish groups
5. Combine and narrow down those groups to four or five.
6. Create a single sentence that summarizes each group of vision ideas.
7. Create a single vision that captures all five groups in a single sentence.

8. Put it on the wall, on mugs, on bulletin boards, on luggage tags, etc.
9. Live it!
10. Put all the groupings of ideas in this journal. Keep every single idea.

Family DNA: Action 2
Defining Our Family Mission Statement

We stand for …

We protect …

We celebrate …

Family DNA:

Refining Our Family Mission Statement

We show that we love God by …

We show that we love others by …

With God's help, we will always …

Jesus says, "He who has ears to hear, let him hear" (Matthew 11:15).

James says, "Faith without works is dead" (James 2:17).

Proverbs says, "When there is no vision, the people perish—chaos rules" (Proverbs 29:18).

Hear the Word of the Lord.

Family DNA: Action 3

Building Core Competencies

Family Competency: 'kam-pe-ten(t)-se
A defining capability or advantage that distinguishes our family from other families.

We distinguish ourselves by ...

- building trusting relationships;
- building each other's strengths;
- becoming leaders in learning and growth;
- inspiring clarity, courage, grit, and gratitude;
- thinking critically and problem-solving;
- communicating clearly and effectively; and
- living with personal responsibility.

Decide as a family how each of these competencies look:

What is excellent?
What is acceptable?
What is tolerable?
What is unacceptable?

Family DNA: Action 4

Sourcing Goodness and Grace

When your family experiences success, you take the credit or you give the credit to someone or something (Thank you, Lord; thank God; or thank my lucky stars, karma, lucky duck, destiny, the universe, etc.).

Who gets the credit for your success?

Who gets the blame for your failure?

Every perfect gift is from God!

What would it look like in your family if you recognized that every good and perfect gift is from God and that His grace covers your failure?

Favor!

> God's anger is for a moment, but His favor is for a lifetime. (Psalm 30:5)

What does it look like when you change "That was lucky" or "What are the odds?" to "God is showing His favor toward us"?

How does reframing the source of goodness as God's favor toward us change our perspective?

How does recognizing God's favor diminish fear?

How does recognizing God's favor create humility? Gratitude?

What is the relationship between "your success" and "God's favor"?

Small Kingdom!
When you make a surprising connection with another person, you'll likely say, "It's a small world."

How would your perspective change if you believe that "It's a small kingdom" instead? In God's story, we constantly discover the connections He has already built into the story. When we follow Him, sometimes, He gives us a little peek at the bigger story.

Wow! It's a small kingdom.

Nothing is wasted in God's economy!
Twelve baskets of leftovers were collected after feeding five thousand families. God's ways are above our ways, but sometimes, He gives us a view from His perspective. With a wink, God shows us how He has connected us to His eternal story and one another.

> He is working all things together for good for those who love him and are living in His story. (Romans 8:28)

Casting your bread on the water is trusting in the one who is writing the story and discovering that you're already in it. There is a place of purpose in God's story for you, your family, and every person in your family. When we find our place in God's story, we reflect His light.

Let your light shine in the world so that they will see your good works and give glory to your Father in heaven. (Matthew 5:16).

Loving others as He has loved us

As we receive goodness and grace from God, we gain the capacity to extend His goodness and grace to others. We are only able to draw from the well that He fills.

As He loves you and you receive grace ...

He becomes the source of your strength;

He becomes the power behind your grit;

He becomes the sustainer of the grace you extend to others;

He becomes your joy in the morning; and

He becomes the hope that carries you through the valley.

Family DNA: Action 5

Check Your Family Fruit

Every family is known for the fruit they produce. No, it's not fruit from an orchard; it's the fruit from the heart. Jesus tells a parable in the Sermon on the Mount about trees bearing fruit.

"You will know a tree by the fruit it produces. Grapes grow on carefully grown vines, not wild bushes. Figs grow on trees, not from thistles. Good trees bear good fruit. Strong pruned vines don't produce terrible grapes. Bad trees and bad vines can't produce good fruit. Every tree that does not produce good fruit will be cut down and thrown into the fire. So listen carefully. You will be known by your fruit" (Matthew 7:15–20).

How healthy is your family fruit? I'm confident that you have some good fruit and some that need your attention. How can your family produce better fruit that gives life?

Good Fruit

How we can be more intentional in producing the "good fruit of the spirit" found in Galatians 5:22–23?

What does this look like in our driveway? Our classroom? Our dorm room? The bleachers? The court? The sideline? The car? Driving in the left lane behind a slow car? Work? Vacation?

Living Faith

Faith is expressed and demonstrated in the following qualities. What do these qualities look like in your family? What steps will you take to make them more evident?

Love

Joy

Peace

Patience

Goodness

Kindness

Gentleness

Self-control

Family DNA: Action 6

Check Navigation, Adjust Trajectory

You move toward excellence with small, intentional steps. You change your trajectory immediately by making small changes today that lead to substantial growth over the long haul. You can start immediately by doing the following:

- **Celebrating the wins, your progress, and your effort**. Only genuine, honest feedback. This is not a participation prize, but sometimes we just need affirmation for stepping into the challenge. Celebrate actions leading to the desired goal.
- **Giving grace in the setbacks.** Failure means we tried. Grace makes room for the grit to try again. There was a sign in our garage over the athletic cubbies, "25 failures, 26 tries."
- **Pursuing excellence, not perfection.** Define the perfect effort not the perfect outcome. In basketball, if you focus on blocking out, then rebounds will follow. If you measure success solely on rebounds, fouls will follow. Celebrate and build habits that support excellence.
- **Find community.** We can't do it on our own.
- **Find the Vine.** It starts with Jesus. He is the only foundation that will not fail in the storm. It continues in the community.

"I am the vine, you are the branches, keep your heart connected to my heart, love others as I have loved you, hide my word in your heart, you will bear so much fruit and your joy will be made full" (John 15:1–11).

Each of the five previous challenges requires that you figure out the "how." This is unique to every family of choice. Figure it out together; be excellent.

Family DNA: Action 7
Reverse Engineer Your Family Legacy

What do you want your family to be known for?

Define the legacy you want to leave behind.

If you reverse engineer that legacy, what are the small steps you can take today that move you in that direction?

Begin with the end in mind. What will you start doing today?

Family DNA: Action 8

Living Out the Greatest Commandment

Jesus was asked, "What is the greatest commandment?" His response was "Love the Lord your God will all your heart, with all your soul, and with all your mind. This is the first and greatest commandment. The second greatest commandment is your response to the first. Love your neighbor as you love yourself. Everything else hangs on these two" (Matthew 22:37–40).

When your family is loving God well, it looks like

When your family is loving others well, it looks like

My prayer for you and your family,
    Know Him.
    Make Him known.
    Know that you're in God's story.

    With all my heart, Dave

The Generous Character of Jesus

The divine and human nature of Jesus is woven throughout my fictional narrative of these true miracles and events found in the four Gospels.

> Jesus was led by the Spirit into the wilderness to be tempted by the devil. After fasting forty days and forty nights, he was hungry. The tempter came to him and said, "If you are the Son of God, tell these stones to become bread." Jesus answered, "It is written: 'Man shall not live on bread alone, but on every word that comes from the mouth of God.'" (Matthew 4:1–4)

Thanks to God for his indescribable grace.

> My grace is sufficient for you. My power is made perfect in weakness. Because of that, I still pursue excellence knowing the truth that even in my weakness the power of Christ and his favor rest on me. II Corinthians 12:9

Turning stone into bread

Is it a sin to eat bread? No. Would it have been a sin for Jesus to turn stones into bread and eat before the end of His forty-day fast? Yes. The temptation was to satisfy a personal carnal need by compromising a spiritual covenant.

Turning stones into bread for the purpose of feeding five thousand people is an entirely different context. Scripture does not elaborate on how the miracle happened; this part of the miracle is creative. The disciples were looking only at horizontal solutions for an impossible problem. There was no money to buy food, no place to buy food, and too many people for "man-sized" solutions. Sending them away was their best option until Andrew spoke up.

It was Andrew who first believed that small gifts in God's hands can feed thousands. Maybe Andrew remembered the torn and empty nets the brothers had when they first met Jesus. He invited the brothers to make one more cast on the other side of the boat. Their boats almost sink because of the miraculous catch of fish. Andrew found the boy with the lunch and brought him to Jesus. Turning stones into bread *could* have been a way Jesus delivered this miracle. It also could have been like manna in the wilderness during the Exodus. No matter how this miracle happened, it originated in humility and the gratitude of a child. This miracle happened while they were giving thanks. It made such a profound impact on the disciples that it is the only miracle recorded in all four Gospels.

He can turn a heart of stone into a heart of flesh, beating for Him and His renown.
The same miracle of turning stone into something living happens every day. It happens for those of us who meet Jesus and release guilt, anger, resentment, fear, loss, and hurt. You don't go from being bad to being good; you go from being dead to being alive.

> I will give you a new heart and put a new spirit in you; I will remove from you your heart of stone and give you a heart of flesh. (Ezekiel 36:26)

> Yes, LORD, walking in the way of your laws, we wait for you; your name and renown are the desire of our hearts. (Isaiah 26:8)

> Beauty from ashes,
> wholeness from brokenness,
> fullness from emptiness. (Isaiah 61:3)

Moms are always moms.
The creative addition to this story of moms getting involved and sharing what they brought is simply undisputable mom behavior.

1. Moms always have a little backup snack hiding somewhere.
2. Moms always make sure every kid has a little something.
3. There were five thousand men on the hillside. How could they find this place without their wives? LOL. Moms were there.
4. Moms are always moms, every community, every country, for all of time.

Jesus takes normal and makes it beautiful.

> He turns water into wine at the wedding feast in Cana. (John 2:1–11)

It wasn't that Jesus just turns water into wine. He makes the best wine the winemaker and guests have ever tasted. This miracle happens all the time, every day, around the globe in France, Spain, Argentina, Australia, and California's Napa Valley. Water and sugar in the grapes ferment over time to produce a variety of flavors based on the soil, altitude, harvest, and process. The crushing and pressing, fermentation and clarification, all culminate in aging and bottling. Jesus just speeds up the process at the wedding feast. This miracle happens every day, but it usually takes months, even years. We've seen that "even the wind and waves obey him." Well, so do grapes and fermentation.

There is nothing wasted in God's economy.
Why did Jesus ask that all the leftovers be collected? There is no explanation or reason given in any of the four Gospel accounts. We simply don't know. We do know that God has purpose and design for everything He does, for every command He gives, for every request He makes. Sometimes we get the why, sometimes we get the

wait. Always, He invites us to trust and follow Him. And as always, He faithfully delivers at just the right time.

Full baskets of grain at the end of *Bread on the Water*
The miracle of filling the empty baskets with the best grain at the end of this story is not found in any ancient manuscript or historical record. This example of a miracle is in line with miracles Jesus has already done. It's in His nature and consistent with His character.

In His ministry, Jesus is generous
He almost sinks their fishing boat and breaks their nets with a miraculous catch of fish.

He almost sinks their fishing boat and breaks their nets again with another miraculous catch of fish.

He feeds four thousand.

He feeds five thousand.

He turns six thirty-gallon stone containers of water into 180 gallons of the best wine at a wedding feast in Cana.

The simple truth of the kingdom of God is found in the sermon on the mount in Matthew.

"Seek first His kingdom and His righteousness,
and all these things will be added unto you," (Matthew 6:33).

What Jesus can do with fish, bread and wine, He can do with fruit! Fruits like love, joy, peace, patience, kindness, goodness, gentleness, and self -control.

The Generous Character of God in the Old Testament

Wisdom in Proverbs

> Trust in the Lord with all your heart. Don't depend on your own understanding, in every way, at all times, acknowledge Him, and He will direct your journey. (Proverbs 3:5–6)

Elisha and the Widow's Oil

God turned a few drops of olive oil into barrels and barrels of oil. There was enough to sell, pay off all her debts, and live off the rest.

> Now the wife of one of the sons of the prophets cried to Elisha, "Your servant, my husband, is dead. You know that he feared the Lord and served Him faithfully. The banker has come to take my two children to be his slaves because we can't pay back the money, we owe him."
>
> And Elisha said to her, "What shall I do for you?" (silence–no answer)
>
> "Tell me what have you in the house?"
>
> And she said, "Your servant has nothing in the house except a small jar of oil."
>
> Then Elisha said, "Go outside, borrow empty vessels from all your neighbors, as many vessels as you can possibly find. Then go into your house and shut the door behind yourself and your sons. Start pouring oil into one of these vessels. And when one is full,

set it aside. Keep filling vessels until your jar of oil
is gone."

She went from him and did exactly as he had
instructed. She shut the door behind herself and
her sons. And as she poured and filled each vessel,
her sons brought her another vessel to her. When all
the vessels were full, she said to her son, "Bring me
another vessel." And he said to her, "There are no
more empty vessels. We have filled every vessel that
we collected." Then the oil stopped flowing. She
came and told Elisha what had happened, and he
said, "Go! Sell the oil and pay your debts, and you
and your sons can live on the rest." (2 Kings 4:4–7)

The size of the miracle was in direct proportion to their obedience.

Manna in the Wilderness
God provided manna every day in the wilderness during the exodus
from Egypt. Forty years of daily provision was faithfully provided.

Jehovah Jireh says to Moses, I will rain down bread
from heaven. This food will be for you and all the
people of Israel. It's your daily bread, we'll call it
manna. Gather enough for your family for today. I
will provide tomorrow's manna tomorrow. On the
sixth day, collect enough manna or two days so you
can rest on Shabbat. Trust me, I am your provider.
(Exodus 16:4–5)

He Is My Portion
Our heavenly Father provides for you exactly what you need at that
moment you need it. This does not mean that it will be the same

for everyone. God knows you. He knows what portion is right for you. Do you trust Him? Will you make this proverb your prayer?

> Give me neither poverty nor riches;
> Feed me with the food that is my portion.
> (Proverbs 30:8)

Kingdom of God Truth

Rejoice in the Lord always; again, I say, rejoice! Let your gentle spirit be known to all people. The Lord is near. Don't be anxious about anything, but in everything pray with a humble and grateful heart, let your requests be made known to God. And the peace of God, which goes beyond all comprehension, will guard your hearts and minds in Christ Jesus.

Finally, friends, whatever is true, whatever is honorable, whatever is right, whatever is pure, whatever is lovely, whatever is commendable, if there is any excellence and anything worthy of praise, wholeheartedly focus on these things. As for the things you have learned from me and seen in me, practice these things, and the God of peace will be with you.

For I have learned to be content in whatever circumstances I am. I know how to get along with little, and I can also live in prosperity; in any and all circumstances I have learned the secret of being satisfied, whether I'm filled or going hungry, both in having abundance and experiencing need. I can do all things through Christ who gives me the strength I need. (Philippians 4:4–12)

The heart of this blessing is contentment and peace regardless of station or circumstance. The blessing of true joy comes out of a relationship with Jesus. There is a direct relationship between following Jesus wholeheartedly and finding joy that is unexplainable, immeasurable, and unstoppable.

Follow me, as I follow Christ. This invitation is one of Paul's most difficult to offer and difficult for us to accept. This is generational discipleship. I promise to follow Jesus; follow me only as I follow Jesus. I promise to place every part of my life under the authority of Jesus, so there is no inconsistency. We won't always get it right, but we can get it more right today than we did yesterday. God's grace is sufficient and redeeming.

Reading the Physical Bible

The words of scripture are God's breath on the page, inspired and guided by the Holy Spirit through its authors. These accounts are accurately preserved from the beginning in the first century.

It is important to read the original verses to ensure we differentiate between what is inspired from what is created.

Harmonization of the Gospels is a Bible study technique I learned at the Cincinnati Bible College during my undergrad studies of the Gospels with R. C. Foster. It is an effective clarifying tool for understanding the perspectives of the four authors and their intended audience. This comprehensive view adds clarity as it eliminates perceived conflicting facts.

Why are there four Gospels with similar and unique details?

When you look at the ministry of Jesus as if it were a house, each author looks at the house from one of the four sides. Some of the stories and details each author writes are unique and other things are similar. They're all looking at the same house, but from a unique perspective. Each author is also writing to a unique audience. It is as if four unique people groups are each standing on the four sides of the same house. The four authors are looking at the same house from different directions. Harmonization is looking from a drone's perspective and including all the details in a single version. Here's the breakdown of vantage points and views.

Matthew 14:13–21—An eyewitness Jewish author writing to a Jewish audience.

Mark 6:30–44—An eyewitness Jewish author writing to a Roman audience.

Luke 9:10–17—He interviewed eyewitnesses, A physician writing to Jews and Romans.

John 6:1–14—A Jewish eyewitness writing to evangelize the whole world.

Matthew 14:13–21 (American Standard Version [ASV])

An eyewitness account of a Jewish author writing to a Jewish audience.

Now when Jesus heard *it*, he withdrew from thence in a boat, to a desert place apart: and when the multitudes heard *thereof*, they followed him 9on foot from the cities. And he came forth, and saw a great multitude, and he had compassion on them, and healed their sick. And when even was come, the disciples came to him, saying, The place is desert, and the time is already past; send the multitudes away, that they may go into the villages, and buy themselves food. But Jesus said unto them, They have no need to go away; give ye them to eat. And they say unto him, We have here but five loaves, and two fishes. And he said, Bring them hither to me. And he commanded the multitudes to sit down on the grass; and he took the five loaves, and the two fishes, and looking up to heaven, he blessed, and brake and gave the loaves to the disciples, and the disciples to the multitudes. And they all ate, and were filled: and they took up that which remained over of the broken pieces, twelve baskets full. And they that did eat were about five thousand men, besides women and children.

Mark 6:30–44 (ASV)

An eyewitness account of A Jewish author writing to a Roman audience.

And the apostles gather themselves together unto Jesus; and they told him all things, whatsoever they had done, and whatsoever they had taught. And he saith unto them, Come ye yourselves apart into a desert place, and rest a while. For there were many coming and going, and they had no leisure so much as to eat. And they went away in the boat to a desert place apart. And *the people* saw them going, and many knew *them*, and they ran together there on foot from all the cities, and outwent them. And he came forth and saw a great multitude, and he had compassion on them, because they were as sheep not having a shepherd: and he began to teach them many things. And when the day was now far spent, his disciples came unto him, and said, The place is desert, and the day is now far spent; send them away, that they may go into the country and villages round about, and buy themselves somewhat to eat. But he answered and said unto them, Give ye them to eat? And they say unto him, Shall we go and buy two hundred shillings' worth of bread, and give them to eat? And he saith unto them, How many loaves have ye? go *and* see. And when they knew, they say, Five, and two fishes. And he commanded them that all should sit down by companies upon the green grass. And they sat down in ranks, by hundreds, and by fifties. And he took the five loaves and the two fishes, and looking up to heaven, he blessed, and brake the loaves; and he gave to the

◅ DAVID W. POINDEXTER ▻

disciples to set before them; and the two fishes divided he among them all. And they all ate, and were filled. And they took up broken pieces, twelve basketfuls, and also of the fishes. And they that ate the loaves were five thousand men.

Luke 9:10–17 (ASV)

He interviewed eyewitnesses, writing down their testimonies
A physician writing to a Jewish and a Roman audience.

> And the apostles, when they were returned, declared unto him what things they had done. And he took them, and withdrew apart to a city called Bethsaida. But the multitudes perceiving it followed him: and he welcomed them, and spoke to them of the kingdom of God, and them that had need of healing he cured. And the day began to wear away; and the twelve came, and said unto him, Send the multitude away, that they may go into the villages and country round about, and lodge, and get provisions: for we are here in a desert place. But he said unto them, "Give ye them to eat." They said, "We have no more than five loaves and two fishes; except we should go and buy food for all this people." For they were about five thousand men. And he said unto his disciples, Make them sit down in companies, about fifty each. And they did so, and made them all sit down. And he took the five loaves and the two fishes, and looking up to heaven, he blessed them, and brake; and gave to the disciples to set before the multitude. And they ate, and were all filled: and there was taken up that which remained over to them of broken pieces, twelve baskets.

John 6:1–14 (ASV)

An eyewitness account of a Jewish author writing to evangelize the whole world.

After these things Jesus went away to the other side of the sea of Galilee, which is *the sea* of Tiberias. And a great multitude followed him, because they beheld the signs which he did on them that were sick. And Jesus went up into the mountain, and there he sat with his disciples. Now the Passover, the feast of the Jews, was at hand. Jesus therefore lifting up his eyes, and seeing that a great multitude cometh unto him, saith unto Philip, Whence are we to buy bread, that these may eat? And this he said to prove him: for he himself knew what he would do. Philip answered him, Two hundred shillings' worth of bread is not sufficient for them, that every one may take a little. One of his disciples, Andrew, Simon Peter's brother, saith unto him, There is a lad here, who hath five barley loaves, and two fishes: but what are these among so many? Jesus said, Make the people sit down. Now there was much grass in the place. So the men sat down, in number about five thousand. Jesus therefore took the loaves; and having given thanks, he distributed to them that were set down; likewise, also of the fishes as much as they would. And when they were filled, he saith unto his disciples, gather up the broken pieces which remain over, that nothing be lost. So they gathered them up, and filled twelve baskets with broken pieces from the five barley loaves, which remained over unto them that had eaten. When therefore the people saw the sign which he did, they said, This is of a truth the prophet that cometh into the world.

I'm In Coaching BEST Inc.

Pursuing excellence in every aspect of life
https://im-in.org/
dpoindexter4@gmail.com

David Poindexter is one of the founding partners and current COO of their 501c3 established in 2007 in Zionsville, Indiana. They've led over one thousand teammates on service adventures in Haiti and Nicaragua over the past twelve years and invested hundreds of thousands of hours in service with local neighbors.

Our Mission

I'm In Coaching Best builds men and women for others. We connect people, schools, businesses, NGOs, missions, and churches to meet genuine needs in our communities and globally. We develop leaders through serving others. We support every teammate in discovering their unique strengths, passion, and purpose.

Our service adventures build servant leaders. Each new adventure is led by students from previous adventures. We carefully calibrate leadership training for inaugural adventures. Our goal is to equip every participant on the team to use their strengths for leading when they get back to their schools and communities and then lead next year's adventure. Coaches partner with students as a team on each service adventure in building leadership skills and purpose. Inspiration and passion become the fuel for growth. We meet genuine needs abroad by coming alongside partners already leading sustainable organizations. We help meet their needs with our teams' hearts, abilities, and strengths. We gain a broader vision and focused purpose.

We build people. We build teams. We build community.

- We lead adventures locally and abroad.
- We can consult with mission teams for leadership development and spiritual formation.
- We can join your team as a mentor.
- We can help you organize and lead your own mission/service/adventure team tailoring everything to exceed your goals

I'm In Coaching Best and the Family on Purpose series are both not-for-profit organizations. It is likely that this book is a gift from a friend. Please consider paying it forward as an investment in other families. A $20 donation provides a book for the next family, or you can buy them as gifts or use them as resources for small groups and family ministries.

This is the link to purchase additional books: QR Code for additional books

This is the link for a ministry support gift: QR Code for making a donation

Recommended Resources:

Common Bible Translations
New American Standard Bible (NASB)
English Standard Version (ESV)
New International Version (NIV)
New King James (NKJV)
The Message (MSG)
The Amplified Bible (AMP)

Online Bible App
Youversion: https://www.youversion.com/the-bible-app/

From friends

"We have had the honor of working with many people and organizations that lead teams to visit our ministry in Nicaragua. There is not one leader that has left a bigger impression than Dave Poindexter. He guides and shepherds the youth he brings straight to the heart of Jesus. He is intentional with his students and just as intentional with every person he comes into contact with here on the field. Dave has made a lasting and indelible impression on those we serve all while lifting up our arms and encouraging us. His warmth, wisdom, and way with words makes anything he does worthy of taking note"

—Scott Esposito, REAP Granada, Nicaragua

"Dave has found an innovative way to draw young people and their families to the relevance of Scripture stories, whetting their appetite for a greater understanding and appreciation of who Jesus is. The messages are relevant to our modern-day lives, challenging families to discuss and find their core values. The stories shed light on the blessings of biblical core values—blessings to both the receiver and the giver, and for the benefit of the culture at large."

—Elizabeth Culp, 5G Prayer Network, Zionsville, Indiana

"If Dave Poindexter is involved, it is well worth doing" is a phrase that I have repeated to many people and this book is another example. I have observed Dave live out these concepts with his family for decades and few do it better.

—Larry McWhorter, former head football coach, Zionsville High, Zionsville, Indiana; I'm In Coach

"Dave Poindexter has been a lifelong mentor for me. By traveling alongside me to Nicaragua and Haiti. I was able to witness firsthand Dave's ability to serve as the hands and feet of God. His words have a profound impact, not just on myself, but on everyone who comes in contact with him. His strongly rooted family values are a testament to living out the Word and putting it into practice daily. His integrity, servant leadership, and devotion to others are integral in every facet of his life."

—Kelly Antcliff, A. D. Zionsville Community Schools, Zionsville, Indiana; I'm In Coach

This page is usually reserved for well-known and influential people who encourage you to read this book. I'm not sure you'll recognize any of the names on this page. These friends are faithful and famous in God's eyes. They are prayer warriors who walk faithfully with Jesus every day and lead humbly in their homes, communities, and ministries across the globe. They continue to be my angel army of prayer warriors standing in the gap for our family and nonprofit organization.

For friends

Thank you.

Brenda, my wife, your pursuit of excellence inspires me daily. Thank you for the margin to study and write. Thank you for walking with Jesus and with me.

Emily and David Floyd, your encouragement and gift launched the Family on Purpose Series and published *Bread on the Water*. This is your bread on the water.

Laura Dunshee, friend, kindred spirit, and the first person to read the draft. I cast my "dough" in your direction and your insight helped me realize it could actually become bread.

Ellie, for sharing lunch finders with girls at Winshape Camp, affirming that being a lunch finder is a true calling and that everyone has a lunch worth sharing.

Keith Ogorek and Author Learning Center, thanks be to God! He is good in you. You inspired confidence in the epic small lessons of following Jesus.

Todd Leyden, by your example, you inspire and encourage me to write and tell my part in God's story.

Shannon Stone, you made this better with your detailed edits, fresh eyes, true heart, and honesty.

The hundreds of people who listened to story ideas as God refined the heart of this project.

Thank you!

WestBow Publishing, you got this project launched.

The 5G Prayer Network, the G is for the grandmas and Pastor Edgar. You are the angel army surrounding our family and ministry. You teach me how to worship and pray every day. Every blessing, all favor and protection are the result of your prayers around the table at Zionville Fellowship and every other place where you are in ceaseless prayer. All things are possible through the one who gives us strength, Jesus.

Image Credits used with permission.

Cover art: a child giving bread and fish to Jesus.
  Dr. Helen O. Williams
Cover image: sunset over the Sea of Galilee
  David, Sarah, and Ben Soper – Israel trip 2017
IGA staff, LeRoy, Illinois, circa 1968
  Becky Eddy Fox and Elizabeth Eddy Kaufman
Two Brothers–a final farewell
  Joseph, Zachary, and Caleb Poindexter
Two Friends hugging at St. Martins School, Brookhaven
  Emily Poindexter Floyd
Mamaw "Anna"–her celebration of life photo
  Papaw Bob Bradley
Brad and nephew, Carson Floyd
  Brenda Poindexter
PapaDex and John David at the Atlanta Aquarium
  Caleb and Jori Poindexter
A donkey with three legs pulling a cart with twelve baskets of wheat
  AI
Camels, nets full of fish, DNA helix
  Getty Images

As We Gather
**Heirloom Boards and Tables
for Gathering Families and Friends.**

In addition to writing stories for families, David is a dedicated craftsman and builder. Having spent 40+ years in the industry, he creates legacy pieces that become magnets for friends and conversation. David uniquely crafts each board and table with care and consideration. Each piece is made from sustainably harvested premium hardwood, making them resilient and durable. As We Gather seeks to bring people together to experience the blessing and joy of community. All proceeds benefit character and leadership development through his nonprofit corporation, I'm In Coaching BEST.

Learn more about *As We Gather*:

ABOUT THE AUTHOR

David W. Poindexter, a creative and entrepreneur, has served youth and families for more than thirty years in education, ministry, and nonprofits. A master's in education and counseling provide a foundation for supporting children and families. He helps people discover their strengths, gifts, and passion. It could be leading mission trips to Haiti and Nicaragua, organizing service projects and soccer camps for refugee communities, or climbing Stone Mountain with grandsons, David's answer to any invitation into adventure is, "I'm in." He and his wife have four daughters and two grandsons, for now.